MW00564911

WALKING
IN THE
SHADOW
OF
FOOTSTEPS

A JOURNEY OF ENLIGHTENMENT

ROYNELL YOUNG

WITH ANITA R. HENDERSON

Walking in the Shadow of Footsteps

Roynell Young
Houston, TX, 77054
RoynellYoung.com

In Association with:
Elite Online Publishing
63 East 11400 South, Suite #230
Sandy, UT 84070
EliteOnlinePublishing.com

Library of Congress: Cataloging-in-Publication Data

ISBN: 979-8454736149 (Amazon)
ISBN: 978-1-7377284-4-3 (Paperback)
ISBN: 978-1-7377284-3-6 (Hardback)
ISBN: 978-1-7377284-5-0 (eBook)

Printed in the United States of America

FREE DOWNLOAD

Don't begin your journey alone.
Tap into my resources for guidance and inspiration as you walk in the shadow of footsteps.

You'll get:

- Affirmations that guide my daily walk
- My morning routine for success
- My "Think Tank" list of must-read books
- My music playlist for inspiration and motivation

Visit www.RoynellYoung.com/lifespurpose
or scan the QR code below

To my wife, Kathleen, and my son Roy Jr.
Thank you for inspiring me to believe in myself and for
supporting me with your love. Without your support, this
book would not have been written.

Praises for Roynell Young

Having invested nineteen years of coaching in the NFL—four years as an assistant and fifteen years as a head coach—I have worked with many outstanding athletes and professionals. This experience adds a degree of credibility to what I know about Roynell Young.

I first met Roynell in the spring of 1980, while evaluating him as a future first-round draft pick for the Philadelphia Eagles. The evaluation was intense, in that we were serious about selecting him as our first pick. Roynell more than passed the test. He was a quality first pick in every category within our evaluation process. From then on, everything Roynell did reinforced my evaluation of him. He has since become the number one, most complete package as a former football player and human being I have ever coached. Only one other athlete I've coached, Pastor Herb Lusk, has come close to doing what Roynell has done with his Pro-Vision.

Roynell has put his heart, soul, and money into proving that BLM (Black Lives Matter) to him! If there was an NFL Hall of Fame category for someone who has provided opportunities and solved serious problems within our African American communities, Roynell would be the first inductee. No one has come close to doing what he has done with Pro-Vision. He does it for unselfish reasons because he cares.

When you read this book, you will recognize where the foundation of his commitment began and discover how it has developed. This book should be a mandatory read for every rookie coming into the NFL. There are so many athletes in the NFL who could do what Roynell has done, especially when you consider the money they are making today.

I hope this book inspires many to follow in his footsteps and motivates them to get involved by doing some of the same things Roynell continues to do within the community.

Coach Dick Vermeil
Former Head Coach, Philadelphia Eagles

Whatever grace ignited Roynell Young's spiritual awakening, we must all be grateful for it. His light shines bright enough to illuminate a whole community. His ideas about the necessity of an ecosystem, his recognition of the complexities of the disadvantaged, and his faith and devotion are what make his work effective. This book is more than a personal story, it is a guide to invest in people and communities.

Angela Blanchard
President Emerita, Baker Ripley
Senior Fellow Watson Institute, Brown University

This book is a must-read, for it is a book of possibility and hope that uplifts and encourages perseverance. It is a blueprint for anyone seeking the path to their calling.

Dr. Roderick Paige
Former U.S. Secretary of Education
Under President George W. Bush

As the Founder of Pro-Vision, Roynell Young has lifted up more than six thousand disadvantaged youth in the impoverished Sunnyside area of Houston through mentoring, character development, and job training programs. His story is as fascinating as it is inspiring, and it is a blessing to us all that he has taken the time to share it with the world.

Jamey Rootes
WSJ/USA Today international bestselling author
Former President, Houston Texans

There are many obstacles on the journey of life. Roynell shares with us how to navigate that journey and explains what matters most in life: people.

Leslie Frazier
Defensive Coordinator/Assistant Head Coach
Buffalo Bills

Foreword

In early 2009, a friend of mine, Will Bowen, asked me to breakfast. He wanted me to consider joining the board of the Pro-Vision organization in the Sunnyside section of Houston. Will said he had been on the board for a number of years and he thought my NBA background would mesh well with the founder of Pro-Vision, Roynell Young, because he had played a decade or so in the NFL. I knew nothing about Pro-Vision, but I was intrigued by Will's depiction of Roy and his vision for serving the most underserved children in Houston.

A couple of weeks later, I went out to Pro-Vision to meet with Roynell. I had never served on a board before, and I had no idea about the Sunnyside community. The school was located seven miles from my house, but was seven million miles from my experiences. On the drive to the campus, the poverty level was overwhelming. Still, I was excited to meet with Roynell, as he had played in Super Bowl XV for the Philadelphia Eagles against my favorite childhood team, the Oakland Raiders. I wanted to quiz him about what it was like to defend the great Cliff Branch, who just happened to be from Sunnyside.

Entering Roynell's office, I was struck by the fact that there was very little football memorabilia in his office. It became apparent early in our conversation that his football career was in the rearview mirror and he had no time for anyone or anything that did not directly impact his mission for Pro-Vision and the young people it served. His passion and devotion to elevating these young people through a loving but disciplined environment shone through. That, along with his focus on a quality education, an emphasis on character development, building up an aquaponic urban farm—because Pro-Vision is located in a food desert—and a long-range goal of providing affordable housing, formed a big vision. From our conversation, it was obvious that Roynell had found his calling in life and that he was looking for people to help him raise the much-needed funding to give these young people the opportunities they deserved.

I became a board member in 2010 and proudly say that Pro-Vision gave me direction in channeling my own philanthropy. Roynell is an incredible leader, smart, passionate, and stubborn when necessary. He sets high standards that he willingly abides by and demands those on his team do as well. He is the true definition of a servant leader, as he has dedicated most of his professional life to helping those who need help the most. His childhood, his own educational path, his NFL experiences, and his singular focus on helping others after leaving the NFL make him a true American hero.

I am honored to know Roy. My admiration for him and all he has accomplished is immense, and I am excited for you to read his book and maybe just be a little more inspired to help those who need it. Great leaders unite and inspire those around them. Roynell has done that for the Pro-Vision/Sunnyside community. My hope for you after reading Roynell's story is that you emulate his passion and determination and set a course for positive change in your own community.

Jeff Van Gundy
ESPN Commentator
Former NBA coach - Houston Rockets, New York Knicks

Contents

Preface

My clock was ticking faster than I realized. Death was imminent. So blinded was I by my determination to finish my fourteenth marathon that I mistook the tightness in my chest as an ill-fitting T-shirt. In 2004, more than a decade after retiring from a nine-year career in the NFL, I ran what became my last marathon. I had taken up running as a way to de-stress. Turns out, it almost killed me.

I had hit the mythical twenty-mile wall that all marathoners know about, when my shirt suddenly felt like it was crushing my chest and torso. The cool January morning air in Houston did little to ease the discomfort, but I finished the race. After finding the courage to tell my wife what was going on with me, I found myself sitting in the doctor's office. Although I did not suffer a heart attack, tests revealed that my left anterior descending artery was ninety-seven percent blocked, a condition commonly known as the widow maker. Thankfully, my Creator knew my work here was unfinished. From that moment, my lifelong tendency to show up small and play it safe melted away and

1

catapulted me with unwavering certainty towards a future I was being led to create, not for myself, but for humanity.

Marathon 2009

Up to that point I had been running from my dark past towards a future I thought had been predetermined to bring light to others through me, an unlikely messenger. I have been the underdog most of my life—from suffering with tuberculosis as a kid to being rejected by my middle school football team—but I found ways to deal with it. What I learned from failure and rejection is that they're just part of the process that leads to success. There is a parable in the Bible that I relate to—the parable of the prodigal son. It's a testament to my life journey, but more important, it is a tale about a life of redemption. In my case, that redemption has resulted in my gratitude for having a second chance.

Each life has a coding that gets revealed over time. At some point, you develop the need to understand your reason for being. Asking, "Why do I exist and what exists beyond the world we know?" consistently throughout your life has the amazing result of leading you to discover your purpose during your time here on Earth. It is not enough to know what your purpose is; you have to use that knowledge because your purpose is inextricably linked to your vision for the future, and that vision defines your success.

My life has been a series of events you wouldn't think would be experienced in the lifetime of a kid who, until age eighteen, rarely ventured outside of my four-block neighborhood in uptown New Orleans, Louisiana. I witnessed all kinds of nefarious activity as a kid, most of it involving violence, which was far too prevalent in my young life. I knew it was bad, yet I was drawn to it, curious about what it could do for me, unafraid of the consequences. I thought I could handle it all and would always be in the winner's seat. I reasoned that my street smarts and my buddies would get me through any situation. I knew the elders within my tight-knit family expected the best of me. They tried to shelter me from the foolishness of the streets as best they could. But still, I fell into the hole. On the one hand, I was a good kid from a decent and respected family. On the other hand, I yearned for the dark, greedy side. That dual existence put me on the road to destruction and caused my parents more headaches than I'll ever know.

Most of us have only about twenty years of childhood and adolescence before we are considered adults. I lived most of those early years in total darkness. I felt abandoned, cut off, and isolated, in part due to my personality, and partly due to the environment I lived in. The spirits of my ancestors watched over me through the violence and trauma I witnessed, but I didn't know that then. The truth is that, in the not-so-distant past, a multitude of poor souls who bore the same blood as I do found themselves in the belly of a slave ship. They held out with the hope that someone like me would show up one day and not waste the sacrifice of their captive life for a moment of self-serving opportunity. Despite my misdirected behavior, they helped guide me back to my Creator on a fateful December night. From the moment of that spiritual awakening, opportunities were presented to me like Christmas presents. I didn't take time to investigate them because they came wrapped in packaging that resembled books and magazines that were easy to ignore. I was a misguided warrior, uninterested in the pursuit of knowledge. Later, those Christmas gifts became precious items that ignited my journey to unearth my purpose, my journey of walking in the shadow of footsteps.

As a kid, I always felt something was guiding my life and watching over me. In an unconscious way, that truth led me out of my adolescent confusion. Because of that, I feel a responsibility to my ancestors to make this world better by my presence here. Since someone was able to hold on and hold out in hopes that I would show up, I've done the same, and when I'm gone, my life will be part of the continuum of the journey started generations ago. In everything I have done and been through, and in the work I do now, I realize the result is bigger than me.

We are taught in the Western Hemisphere to think about self first. We pride ourselves on being "self-made," but no one truly reaches the destination of success alone. In other cultures and communities, it is about the whole, not the parts, the group, not the individuals, because within the group there is power. But power is not for self-aggrandizement. Power, instead, should be used to uplift the lowly, to shed light on the darkness, and to make right the wrongs inflicted upon the least of us. That can be seen clearly in this current moment, when a bridge between the old and the new way of leading change in our communities is at a desperate intersection. In fact, change and transition are a continuum, not a destination. From the Underground Railroad to the Civil Rights Movement to Black Lives Matter, I celebrate and honor all the advances made to further the causes of Black people, those living in poverty, and other rejected populations. Yet, the voices of the ancestors are calling for humanity to rise up and tap into our better angels. I accept the call.

When Michael Brown was killed in Ferguson, Missouri, in 2014, the people in that community protested for almost four hundred days. They brought light to the long-standing reality of Black men and boys being killed by police and the predictable and frustrating result of no charges being filed against the police officers. Their voices shed light on the disproportionate representation of white people in positions of power within local governments making decisions for majority Black populations. Eventually, the protests died down, the media pivoted away from it, and the rest of the country went back to business as usual, but CORE (Community Organized Relief Effort) and Black Lives Matter were committed. They worked behind the scenes to make change happen. The message of Black Lives Matter took off and gained global attention again in 2020 when the entire world was shut down and people all over the world were cooped up because of COVID-19. Stuck at home, they weren't distracted by all the other news and entertainment. At that time, they were antsy for something to do.

When all the entertainment, sports, and other titillating diversions were removed, people were forced to look in the mirror. By the summer of that year, they were at the starting line, ready for something to pounce on. They got it with the murders of Ahmaud Arbery, George Floyd, Breonna Taylor, and Rayshard Brooks. That's when the explosion happened and people got "woke." I hope the modern-day movement towards civil and human rights has built the bandwidth to sustain its voice and its power. My fear is that the objectives of the protests become lost in the predictable apathy that engulfs a society in the aftermath of civil unrest. To prevent that kind of destructive outcome, people have to be willing to fight for their own liberation. As history has demonstrated, the fight for equality is an emotional endeavor that can be heart-rending and depressing. It takes a concerted effort and a level of dedication and longsuffering to see that commitment to fruition. Those who are in the fight from a righteous standpoint cannot concede. They must prevail.

My role in this modern-day movement is to build an institution to be a positive influence in the community. That's what Pro-Vision represents. I don't have an overwhelming need to be heard, and I definitely do not need to be put on a pedestal or receive any accolades. But if somebody seeks me out and thinks I can add value to the discussion, I'll do what I can to make an impact. As the old folks say, "Talk is cheap." Actions speak louder than words when the conversation is about community enhancement and furthering the footprint of Black and disenfranchised people in this world. My goal is to follow through on the rhetoric and take action towards true, lasting, empowering change.

Realizing my purpose was the beginning of my journey, the wake up. Living out my purpose has been a continuous process to clean up, stand up, and show up, resulting in enlightenment for me. The journey has not been easy, but it has been worth every step and misstep. Along the way, I have transcended my environment and become an active vessel of change for others. Taking agency back over my life has allowed me to put into perspective who I am, what I am, and what I should be doing with my time here on earth.

My life has been like that of the prodigal son. I've experienced the good, the bad, and the ugly. I have left home, enjoyed the pleasures of life, found myself in a lowly state, and then realized my ancestors and my Creator had more in store for me. Thankfully, I found my way back home, back to myself. This reflection of my life is a snapshot of that journey.

Fourth-grade play. Me with younger brother, Brian Young (right)

A PRODUCT OF MY ENVIRONMENT

Getting from one end of the 2100 block of Delachaise Street to the other was like running through an obstacle course. At each corner, and everywhere in between, were elders and adults who watched and ruled everything that happened. That was my village while growing up in the 1960s, and it provided a nurturing safety net that protected me from the harsh realities of the world beyond. Yet, there was always something inside me pushing against that protection, hungry to break out and explore, desperate to prove something to myself or experience some imaginary version of worthiness. My unceasing curiosity eventually inflicted unnecessary hardships that took me through the university of hard knocks.

Many of the values I was raised with seemed to be totally false—do unto others, give and it shall be given, knock and the door shall be opened. They all sounded good, but life showed me things don't always work that way. You do not always get good in return for giving it, and not every door opens when you knock. Over time, I discovered life is not black and white; it is not right and wrong; it's not a straight line.

When I was eleven years old, the community influence was strong enough to shield me from the influences outside of the uptown Twelfth Ward community where I grew up on Delachaise and Saratoga Streets. My parents and the other adults around me cared enough to do what was necessary to keep me on the straight and narrow. So I did what good kids did—sort of. I had an outer façade of goodness, but really, I was living a dual existence. For the most part, I did what was expected of me. I said, "Yes, ma'am, no ma'am." I went to church. But every moment of free time fed my imagination and curiosity about other things. Even as a kid, I wanted to experience what I thought were the best parts of life. The only problem was that my idea of what was so great was kind of warped. Some would say I was a wayward kid. I would say I was precocious and curious. No matter how good I was, there was always a temptation to try something new, something different. So I pushed the boundaries many times and that led me to some not-so-good places.

Early on, I realized I was in a unique, vibrant city, and its underbelly attracted my curiosity. For example, in New Orleans, around Mardi Gras, the flambeau carriers walked the streets with torches that provided light for the colorful parade floats. This practice began in the 1850s, for a practical purpose, when enslaved Africans and free people of color were charged with lighting the way, as it were. Over time, the flambeaux turned into something demeaning. Black men would dance and perform while twirling their lighted sticks down Canal Street, Bourbon Street, and other parade routes. No longer a practical part of the parades, the flambeaux became a spectacle. Today, it's appropriated as a source of entertainment that exaggerates the culture of Black people. Even white people carry torches now, which further characterizes the historical context of it as a joke.

Back in the day, my parents and the elders would line the Mardi Gras parade routes in our neighborhood and comment about how the flambeaux looked like clowns—unkept, wearing smocks and bandanas to protect themselves from the kerosene, almost menacing as they danced down the street carrying on, nearly to the point of buffoonery. In fact, one could say they looked like a strange version of the Klan, except they were clownish with their elaborate, rhythmic dancing. Many of the guys had recently come out of prison, so they were considered gutter types. The more they clowned and danced, the more white people threw money at them, and that just made the elders even madder. For some reason, the mystique and flamboyance of these dancers resonated with me. I wanted to be like them. They were outside the boundaries of the norm. They were outlaws and rebels, and as a kid, that convoluted performance drew my attention. Knowing what I know now, those guys were a linkage to my ancestral past, to the revelry and celebration of nineteenth-century Congo Square, back when jazz was being created. In a perverted and unconscious way, I was trying to reattach the roots to my African ancestry, which had been severed.

When I learned where those guys went to get their torches, I set out in search of my own. My eldest sister, Michelle, found out what I was doing, and she was livid because, to her, that was the most sacrilegious, disrespectful thing I could do to embarrass my family. She told my mom, who intercepted me and thwarted my attempt to be a flambeau. That failed attempt only heightened my desire for the dark side. I didn't resort to the violence of my surroundings, but what I did—things like smoking cigarettes and trying my hand at street tattoos—was enough to let me know there was a lot to like about the wild side. As much as I could, at twelve, I partook in all the city had to offer, and that was a lot.

Then, as it is now, New Orleans was like a prostitute, in that rich men came to be with her at night, but they didn't want to be seen with her in the day. People come to the city from all over the world to take advantage of its reputation. They do things in New Orleans they would never do at home because they are "respectable people." The sad thing is New Orleans has for so long positioned itself in a way that has made it hard to change that reputation. Maybe some don't even want to. Since its founding, New Orleans has been a city filled with romance, mystery, and violence, the ingredients of a metropolitan gumbo. Like a good gumbo, that blend needs a great roux. Without the roux, it's just soup. For New Orleans, violence is the roux.

My mom, Joyce, knew she had her hands full with me, her third born, because I was the one kid who pushed the boundaries, the one she had to account for. My siblings did what was expected, but not me. Even if I had to take a beat down for going outside the rules, I was going to do it. A combination of Oprah Winfrey, Stacey Abrams, and Maxine Waters all rolled into one, my mom loved all six of her kids, but she was tough. "Don't mess with Miss Joyce," the kids in our neighborhood would say. People tiptoed around my mom to avoid her temper and her wrath. Years later, I realized she was a frustrated genius.

As a young woman, she was offered a scholarship to attend the University of Michigan to study pre-med and play basketball, but she let it go. I never knew why. Around that time, she met my father Wallace. He was her knight in shining armor, her chance to enter into motherhood and to nurture and coach her kids, who grew up to be productive, responsible citizens. She was a stay-at-home mom for a few years, then did some factory work, and later worked at the school cafeteria. None of those jobs were a career for her. They were just short-term work to help make ends meet. Mom was a sharp lady, the de facto mayor of our neighborhood. When people complained to the city, she was the one who wrote letters to get things done. Everyone took her seriously, and that was enough to keep us all in line, except me.

My sister, Whylene, who we called Pie, was a new-and-improved version of my mother. She was a go-getter and a do-gooder. Maybe that's why she and my mom clashed on occasion; they were so much alike. One day, Pie ratted me out to my mom when she saw me on the corner with some older boys who were teaching me how to smoke. We were taught to be proud of our family and our family name and never bring shame to it. So when Pie saw me on that corner, I knew I couldn't buy her silence. When my mom found out about it, she was not happy. I denied it like my life was on the line.

"So you want to be a thug, huh? You want to hang out with the lowlifes?" my mom said. I was speechless. I knew the right answer, but I also knew my behavior had shown the opposite. She approached me with a carton of cigarettes she had bought. "You want to smoke?" she asked, almost threateningly. "Okay, you're going to learn how to smoke."

When she lit up the first cigarette, my heart began to pound inside my chest as if she was forcing me to drink a toxic mixture of bleach and turpentine. I screamed and squirmed and almost ran away, but I knew running would only make her madder. She forced the cigarette between my tightly closed lips and yelled at me to puff. The smell of the smoke was suffocating, and it burned my eyes. After a few seconds passed, and I refused to take a puff, she tapped me on the butt with a belt and said, "No, smoke!" I puffed and blew and puffed and blew until I got down to the filter. Then, she lit another cigarette and shoved it

14

between my lips, forcing me to smoke once again. Eventually, I started choking and coughing up phlegm until I finally said, "Stop, stop, I can't breathe!" Still, she told me to puff, puff, puff. As soon as I took a breath, she stuck another cigarette in my mouth. Finally, my savior arrived.

"Okay, okay, that's enough," my dad said. As always, he rescued me. "The boy has learned his lesson. Go on and clean yourself up, son."

My eyes were full of water and I could barely breathe. Meanwhile, my brothers and sisters stood in the distance, watching, undoubtedly thinking my mother had nearly killed me. Sadly, that was not the first or the last time that kind of scene played out in our household. Thankfully, there was always someone to save me from myself.

My dad was a charmer who solved problems with stories. His nickname was "Watch My Feet" because he was a dancer. Unlike most dads, he never spanked us. Whenever I did something wrong, he would just say, "Son, I'm disappointed in the choice you made." That hurt me more than any whipping. His mother was also an amazing human being. My grandmother, Stella Gibbs, had a sort of hero worship syndrome with him. He was her pride and joy, the baby of three boys, and he returned her love with an idyllic, nurturing respect. She fussed over him endlessly. As a result, my dad grew up as a confident, intact man, and he brought that persona to our family as the head of the household. After my mom and dad divorced, he remarried. My brothers and sisters and I would meet him on Fridays at the landmark Gumbo House restaurant on Louisiana Avenue and Danneel Street, right around the corner from our house. He always had a white envelope full of money for us to give to Mom. He would talk to each of us and give us advice and allowance.

All I ever wanted to be was my dad. That's how much I admired him. When he died in 2001, I was forty-four years old and a father myself. A lot of young boys attended his funeral. They were the saggy-pants-wearing, nine-millimeter-toting types from the 'hood. On the exterior, they looked menacing and intimidating, but for some reason, my dad had connected with them over the years. He had always been good at developing relationships with people from different walks of life, and he had developed strong relationships with them to the point that they trusted him and accepted his advice. Those guys came to his funeral and cried like babies because of the caring and concern he had shown them. Their hero, and mine, was gone. Seeing those guys there was both a comedy and a sad commentary because they were these big, burly guys crying like two-year-old children who had lost a pacifier. They loved my dad, maybe not in the same way I did, but they loved him and admired him, and they knew they would miss him.

That kind of impact made an impression on me and I wanted to become that for others. To this day, my dad's influence shows up in the work I do at Pro-Vision. As I work with young men and women, I see myself in them, which allows me to relate to them. I know *how* they are thinking and sometimes I know *what* they are thinking because I'm an old-school knucklehead, so there is very little they can pull over my eyes. They cannot imagine that I was once eleven or fourteen or eighteen. I have already been there and done that. Not only do I know what *they* know, but I also know what *I* know, and that is the beauty of the journey of life. I hope the kids I work with see me as an example of someone they can relate to. I hope they see me as someone who has learned the lessons of life and is freely sharing those lessons so they don't have to learn from the university of hard knocks. That is called wisdom. You cannot rush it. You have to earn it.

My schooling led me from parochial school to public school. As a first-grader at Bethlehem Lutheran School on Washington Avenue, I was the valedictorian of my class. I flourished there, and my teacher loved me. Miss Frazier was caring, nurturing, and attentive. She thought I was brilliant, and she made learning fun. That brought a sense of pride to my life and led me to become the star pupil of the class of about a dozen kids. The classroom was orderly, and it was the perfect environment to enrich each student's aptitude for learning, but even that wasn't enough to drown out the realities of life outside the walls of the school.

There are moments in life when major events happen and you remember exactly where you were when you got the news. When I walked into the church sanctuary at school one chilly day in November, I immediately knew something was wrong. My eyes scanned the room to see teachers visibly shaking and crying. None of the students had a clue what was going on, but we knew it must be serious. When the headmaster announced over the loud speaker that President John F. Kennedy had been assassinated, all of us kids were devastated. As young as we were, we knew who the president was, and we knew that him being killed was a bad thing. We were sent home.

I don't recall what happened in the following days and weeks, but that single event changed the trajectory of my life. After the JFK assassination, the entire racial climate changed in America, and that put a damper on many small businesses, including my Uncle Nick's carpentry business. I later learned Uncle Nick had been paying the tuition for my brother and sister and me to attend the school. As things changed, the money no longer came in from his business like it had, so he couldn't sustain the expense.

With our benefactor low on funds, we had to go to a public school. I didn't know what was in store for me at this new school. Part of me was confused because everything seemed different. In parochial school, we wore uniforms, and our days were more regimented. Public school was a world of difference from Bethlehem Lutheran. The first Thomy Lafon School was built in the late 1800s. It was named for a free man of color who had been a businessman, schoolteacher, and philanthropist in New Orleans. During the Robert Charles race riot of 1900, a white mob burned down the school. Years later, it was rebuilt in the heart of the Magnolia Projects, one of the most notorious public housing areas in town. By the time I arrived there as a student, the school had suffered the fate of the surrounding low-income area, having become run down and in need of repair.

For my siblings and me, traversing the four-block area between our house and the school was more than a notion due to the pervasive violence in the projects. So dangerous was my short walk to school that I would have to cross Louisiana Avenue before I could exhale. That was my new reality, and that is where

I lost myself. I went from a class of twelve kids to a class of about thirty-five. I realized early on that the kids who sat in front of the class got the instruction and attention, but those in the back got lost. Unfortunately, the teacher placed me in the back.

My mom was a working woman and did the best she could to engage and enhance my educational experience, but her efforts were not enough to counter the culture shock I experienced when taken out of the parochial school. She assumed I was a model student because I had been at Bethlehem. However, throughout most of my public schooling, I felt extremely unprepared and disconnected. As a result, I became an average student who consistently underperformed. Still, I had a curiosity about and fascination with words. Although I wasn't a great speller, I loved to discover the etymology of words. In my early schooling, my academic performance could be best described as mediocre. In the larger class, I could hide behind the antics of the other students, and there were a lot of hijinks going on.

I learned things at that school I had not been exposed to in parochial school, such as might is right and sometimes the bad guy wins, tough lessons I learned while serving as a crossing guard in fourth grade. That role empowered me and other kids to ensure our fellow students crossed the street safely and behaved themselves as they arrived and left the school grounds. I was a de facto traffic cop, and it felt good. Imagine a fourth-grader doing that job. I excitedly attended the orientation, where the trainer convinced us we would be an extension of the local police. They even went as far as teaching us how to take down license plate numbers and write down any nefarious activities we noticed while on duty. The roughnecks who attended the school thought that position was corny and cliché, but I didn't care. I was determined to gain notoriety and serve my community in some small measure.

Every year, between Thanksgiving and Christmas, the school gave each student a big, beautiful red apple and a juicy navel orange as a treat. One sunny but chilly afternoon, I was at my post and I stashed my fruit, one in each of my coat pockets, and proceeded to carry out my duties as a crossing guard. Out of nowhere, two older boys appeared behind me. One took out a pen knife and put it to my side. "Give me your apple and your orange, or I'm gonna stab you," he said. Without hesitation, I obliged. I watched them as they left me, and walked from one student to the next, pointing that knife and relieving them of their apple and orange. They eventually scattered from the schoolyard and melted back into the projects.

I proceeded to the program sponsor to turn in my flag and badge. "I quit!" I said. The injustice I witnessed that day was unexpected and demeaning. I was at the mercy of a bunch of thugs who had no right to be there, yet had spread fear among my schoolmates and walked away with bags full of items that didn't belong to them. I had to watch it all, despite the fact that I had been placed in a position of authority, which essentially amounted to nothing. That experience was an early underpinning that awakened in me a lifelong crusade for justice and treating people fairly.

It didn't take me long to realize the students at Lafon School were different, tougher. They were sometimes loud and rambunctious, disorderly and undisciplined. Even though I knew their behavior was raw and unacceptable to adults, there was something about it that drew me in, so I watched and learned.

Essentially, I was learning gangster stuff, how to be a thug. Academics didn't fit into that. Interestingly, I fit in well with the "in crowd" and integrated my previously sheltered experience into this new reality. It was an easy transition because I didn't have the oversight of teachers who could focus on me and my needs. They had too much other stuff to concern themselves with. Plus, I noticed that, in public school, the bad kids got all the attention. I guess there was something inside me—inside those bad kids as well—that craved attention. Despite my increasingly bad behavior and my slipping grades, I still had an interest in learning, but I had to hide it. Sadly, my voracious interest in reading and soaking up knowledge went into a deep freeze.

I fell further into the learning abyss one spring day at school. All the kids had run out of class at the end of the day, as usual. Like other third-graders, we couldn't wait to leave the schoolhouse to walk home, stopping at my favorite sweet shop to buy integrated cookies—the sandwich kind with a vanilla cookie on one side, a chocolate cookie on the other side, and cream filling—along with a giant cola to celebrate the end of the school day. As soon as I hit the sidewalk, I realized I had forgotten my notebook, so I ran back inside to get it. As I approached the classroom, I heard the whispering voices of two teachers.

"He's a smart kid, but I wish his mother would dress him better," one said. "He's always so sloppy."

The other teacher agreed. "Yes, if someone would work with him on his spelling, he could probably be a much better student."

As I stood in the doorway eavesdropping, I wondered who they were talking about. My mind raced through the faces of my classmates. Really, they could have been talking about anyone. But then, something they said let me know who the student in question was. They whispered the name Young, but it didn't click in my mind who they were talking about until I heard "Roynell." They were talking about me. I was shocked. I was hurt. I could not believe these two teachers, who I had admired, were talking about me in this way. *Dammit, that's why I'm here, for you to help me*, I thought. These were two adults tasked with helping kids learn and be their best, yet they were gossiping about me like I was a criminal. Words have the power to uplift and to heal. Words also have the power to hurt. Their ill-spoken words had cut me to the core.

After hearing those teachers talking about me like that, my intellectual curiosity completely shut down. That day, I decided, *To hell with school. I'm gonna wild out*. And that was exactly what I did. I became disconnected and aloof, which led to a lot of poor choices that negatively impacted me. My interest in learning was absent throughout the remainder of my schooling until ninth grade. Mediocrity became my best friend for a while. I took the path of least resistance, not knowing that, in the long run, I would have to pay an even higher price.

With my slacking academic performance, I discovered something new about myself. Each day on the playground, the boys would play pick-up sticks. Each person would toss a stick, a branch we broke off a nearby tree, on the ground. One person would pick up the stick and run, and the other guys chased him around the

22

playground. It was a cross between tackle football, wrestling, and X Games. The guy with the stick had to outrun the others and fake them out by dashing back and forth. The object was to hold the stick as long as possible. As long as you had the stick, the others could trip you, punch you, tackle you, whatever. Everything was fair game, and it was brutal. That's when I discovered I was physically gifted.

Whenever I had the stick, I was untouchable. I could outrun them all, faking them out from one corner of the playground to the next. No one could ever touch me. One day, this kid, who was quite a bit bigger than I was, had the stick and was running. I tackled him onto the cement. It was a solid hit and he fell to the ground with a loud thud. His face smashed into the gravel so hard everyone on the playground stopped what they were doing. The guy probably had a concussion and should have been rushed to the hospital. When he got up, he was groggy and clearly shaken. His friends rushed over to pick the gravel out of the side of his face. I just stood there and watched. I wasn't cocky. I didn't boast. There was no squabble, no ruckus. I just had a knowing, an awareness that I was physically superior, and everyone else did too. That day, I became a legend.

I had no idea of the value nor the importance of this newly discovered gift. In fact, it kind of surprised me because I was a late bloomer, a small kid, a runt all the way through my sophomore year in high school. My small size bothered me when I was younger, but I never let it stop me from trying to do all the stuff the bigger guys did. When I went out for my middle school football team, I was turned down, not because I couldn't perform on the field, but because they didn't have a suit to fit me. My middle school PE teacher, Mr. Baker, a Trinidadian with a booming, opera-singer voice, was the first to crush my dream of playing football. After paying the fee to play on the team, I went to practice and was ready to throw down with the other guys. After an hour or so of play, however, I noticed I was the only one on the field wearing shorts and a T-shirt. Everyone else was sporting a uniform, so I approached Mr. Baker to ask about my uniform.

Mr. Baker took me to the side and explained, "Let me tell you something, son. You're too small. We don't have a suit to fit you," he said.

I was confused, not sure what that had to do with me actually playing ball. I figured they could pull together something that looked like a regular uniform, and that would be good enough for me.

He continued, "Listen, there's a good chance something could happen to you because you're so small. I couldn't bear to tell your parents that you got seriously injured. I just can't take that chance."

I didn't know or care enough to appreciate his concern. All I wanted to do was play ball. What I lacked in size I made up for in grit, and I thought that was enough to make a difference on the field. He had crushed my spirit and I walked home crying, cussing, and fussing to myself, determined to prove Mr. Baker wrong.

When I got home, I told my mom what had happened, and I could tell she felt sorry for me. She was sympathetic and encouraging, but she was also a realist. "It's okay, Roy," she said. "You know, some things aren't meant for everybody." I appreciated her concern, but I was frustrated, and that made me dead set on proving Mr. Baker and my mother wrong.

That experience developed in me an appetite for fairness, equity, empathy, and justice. Those ideals evolved as the result of being denied. Still, my natural ability had to develop in other ways outside of organized sports. I went back to playing sandlot football, where I wowed all the bigger kids with my moves and my toughness. Not long after that, I tested positive for tuberculosis and ended up taking medication for three years. In all likelihood, TB was the cause of my small body size. Thankfully, the medication and the support of my family thwarted any lifelong ill effects. The summer before my ninth-grade year, I stayed with my grandmother in Thibodeaux and experienced a remarkable growth spurt. Out of nowhere, I went from being a runt to becoming a full-fledged athlete. Little did I know the gift of athletic prowess would take me to places I never dreamed of and lead me to an unexpected place in life.

Like most African American kids, the women in my life, such as my mom, my grandmothers, and my aunts, were great influencers with larger-than-life personalities. If the men were the ones who brought home the bacon, the women were the ones who put the icing on the cake. They were the engine that kept life moving, the closers who made everything right. These women represented dependability and stability for me. They were the glue that held my life together and established a moral baseline for living. Both strong and sensitive, my sheroes provided the emotional and social insights to help me process life as a human being.

My mom's mother, Bertha Lawson, who we called Grandma Sis, was a city girl with a husky voice. She was legendary for her cooking. People would come from all over New Orleans to purchase one of her "suppers," a plate of fried chicken or red fish with all the fixin's, or a big bowl of gumbo. I'm not sure why, but I didn't have a sense of closeness with her. I knew she loved me and my siblings, but there was a distance I couldn't put my finger on. Even still, I was grateful to have her in my life, and happy she lived so close by. She lived across the street from us, in a double shotgun house, where she occupied one side and my dad's mother, Stella Gibbs, lived on the other. That house was the heart of the village for me.

Stella Gibbs, Herbert Young,
Wallace Young, and Darnell Young

26

Grandma Gibbs was the woman who breathed life into me in terms of my emotional and spiritual development. She was my savior, the one who taught me how to love. She was a proud, dignified woman from Thibodaux, Louisiana. When my mom would have to go to work early, Grandma Gibbs would come over to fix breakfast for all of us kids, then braid the girls' hair, and make sure we got to school on time. She did all of that before she went off to work as a housekeeper for a Jewish doctor and his family in uptown New Orleans. The family she worked for, the Heartstreams, actually got a two-for-one deal with her because she not only cleaned their house, but she also took care of their kids. I still don't know how she managed to do it all, but she did.

Grandma Gibbs was a woman of honor. She took great pride in her credit. From paying her dues at the Masonic Lodge to paying off her line of credit at the Godchaux and Maison Blanche department stores, she had what she called triple-A credit. She didn't carry any long-term debt. I learned from her that your credit speaks to your character. She had only a third-grade education, but she had a PhD in love, and that came through with the fierce care and protection she demonstrated towards her family. Grandma Gibbs was the epitome of love and I always felt her warmth, no matter what missteps I made in life.

I have also been blessed to have a lot of examples of great men in my life—my father, my uncles, especially Uncle Nick, coaches, and so many others. They were examples of how to live, how to be, and how to impact the lives of others. Throughout my childhood, I was very aware of the importance of having these men in my life, even if I did not always show it, tell them, or behave in the most appropriate ways. I did value their presence. I always wanted to be the kind of positive influence for others that those men were to me. As a kid, I had no idea how to do that. It was just something that started deep down in my soul and grew over time, thanks to those positive male influences.

All these men shaped my young mind and helped me realize what a man is supposed to be. They showed me a different side of manhood, an aspirational perspective that wasn't presented in the streets of my neighborhood. Each of them was imperfect in some way, and I think that was part of the appeal for me. I could tell they had been through some things, and those things made them who they were. They had awakened in their own ways and had cleaned up their act. What I saw before me were strong, self-assured men who cared for others. I wanted to be that kind of role model, but it would be years before I would stand in that position.

One of the most influential men in my young life was my grandmother's brother, Roynell Lawson, who we called Uncle Nick. I am his namesake. A complicated and interesting man, he was one of my heroes because he was his own man, free in his mind, militant. He thought on a different level than everyone else in our family. He had joined the Nation of Islam in the 1930s and, as a conscientious objector, refused to serve in World War II. As a result, he spent seven years in Leavenworth Penitentiary, which was a light sentence because, back in the day, they could have lynched him. A Black man refusing to do what the government wanted him to do was a dangerous thing. After serving his time, he became a recluse and didn't come around the family much. It seemed his behavior had created a shroud of shame for our family and in the neighborhood. People whispered about him and kept their distance, but Uncle Nick kept on being himself. I knew he was peculiar, yet I admired him.

Uncle Nick was magical with his hands and could fix anything. He was a tradesman who refinished hardwood floors in a lot of the fine houses that lined St. Charles Avenue. He was so good at what he did that his talent was in great demand, and he taught me his trade when I was about fourteen years old. I was a good apprentice, so good in fact that I eventually had a crew working for me. On the days when I visited Uncle Nick, I sat in the window of his shotgun house and eavesdropped on conversations he had with his buddies as they argued over issues of the day. They sat on his back porch and had rich debates about Black history and the contributions of people like Joe Louis, Paul Robeson, Langston Hughes, and Marcus Garvey.

Uncle Nick was autodidactic and a voracious reader who had bookcases filled with newspapers and books that he devoured. When I saw him sitting quietly in his overstuffed chair on his back porch, gaining pleasure from just reading, I thought, *That's not normal. Why is my Uncle Nick so weird?* Knowledge was his thing, even more important than a formal education, as far as he was concerned, but he did value education. He knew the power of it, which is why he had paid for myself, my sister, and my two brothers to attend Bethlehem Lutheran School, something I didn't know until I was in college. Even though he was not big on the structure of the educational system, he made sure our generation had a fair start in our lifelong learning journey.

Admittedly, I have fallen into his shadow. Maybe I'm trying to imitate him. I have become the Uncle Nick for my nieces and nephews. They talk about me like we used to talk about him.

They whisper when they're around me, and I kind of like it. It connects me to my uncle. In all my years coming up, I could not put my finger on one single thing that made Uncle Nick peculiar. Now I know. He was strange because he was operating in an entirely different realm from everyone else. His experiences—most of which I never knew about—had caused him to wake up, and then he had cleaned himself up. He didn't have to be bombastic or obnoxious to let people know he was a changed man. He was committed to living the life he had chosen. He simply was who he was, his authentic self, and that was enough for him. It was enough for me.

High school prom

Early college days

Going into the Darkness

In New Orleans, Halloween was a fun time. Fireworks were part of the celebration, but were illegal in the city in the 1960s, however, that didn't keep kids like me from getting our hands on a few, not to light up, but to make a few bucks. I have always been a bit of an entrepreneur, even as a kid, and on a particularly warm Sunday afternoon, when I was about eleven years old, my buddy TC and I hopped the ferry and went across the Mississippi—"over da river" as we would say—into the small neighborhood of Algiers and then into Jefferson Parish, where there was an abundance of fireworks. We headed back uptown and decided to set up shop, hoping to find lots of customers and make some fast money.

Standing on the corner of Louisiana Avenue and St. Charles Avenue, where the iconic street cars pass the huge Victorian mansions, we must have looked like a couple of misfits with our brown paper bag full of fireworks. After about ten minutes of looking around for just the right character to make our low-voiced pitch to, a guy I recognized from our neighborhood walked up to us. We called him Dirty Red, and he was an okay guy, so I figured he was safe to sell to. He knew the code of the streets and wouldn't rat us out to the cops, or so I thought. However, TC did not like him. "I don't trust this guy," he said. I ignored him and proceeded to make the sale.

"What you guys got in the bag?" asked Dirty Red, hands deep inside the front pockets of his too-short denim jeans. I'm pretty sure he would have bought whatever we had in that bag as long as the price was right.

Looking over my shoulders casually—left, then right—I opened the crumpled bag to show him our stash of fireworks. We had fireworks of every kind—Black Cats, Roman candles, sparklers. You name it, we had it. He reached inside, grabbed a handful of Black Cat firecrackers, and then handed TC a moist, dirty dollar bill. Without so much as a thank you, he turned to walk away. I called after him, trying not to attract attention from the passersby on the busy uptown street. "Look man, whatever you do, do not light those things around us. Get as far away from here as you can before you light 'em up." He flipped his hand in the air, waving me away, as he shuffled down the street. When he was less than twenty paces from us, we saw the smoke, and then, like the sound of popcorn from a street vendor, the noise came—crack, crack, pop, crack! *Dammit! He did it anyway!* I thought.

Dirty Red took off running, leaving the firecrackers exploding on the sidewalk. Almost immediately, blue lights and sirens started coming down the street. TC and I took off running in the opposite direction of our foolish customer. We ran through the streets of New Orleans like we had stolen something. I saw my life flash in front of me. All I could hear was the good advice I had received from my elders. "Be careful the company you keep." As we rounded the block, I made it to the street I lived on, Delachaise Street. *Only three blocks to go*, I thought. We ran past an apartment complex. *Oh boy, I'm almost home free.* I was so certain we would reach my house safely that my mind began to drift, and I wondered what I would watch on TV that night. Despite my wandering mind, my heart beat faster than I had ever felt it beat, and my legs moved even faster than that. We ran and ran until we rounded the corner about two blocks from my house, then we dashed behind a big oak tree to catch our breath.

Huddled down close to the ground, I said to TC, "Man, we have to ditch this bag. I know that's all our product, but we have to take a loss." TC was so out of breath he couldn't respond, so I took that as his agreement and decided to toss the bag as soon as we passed a reasonable dumping spot. Hearing sirens in the distance, we took off running again.

Just as we were finally free of the evidence, four police cars descended on us from every direction. In no time, TC and I were pinned against a rickety wooden fence by one of the cars. The police car eased slowly forward until the bumper pressed against our knees and we doubled over on the hood, screaming and crying, not because we were scared or ashamed of ourselves, but because it just seemed like the right thing to do. One white officer slowly exited the car, walked up to us, and proceeded to taunt and interrogate us with the idea of breaking us down to gain a confession.

"You boys been selling fireworks?" the officer asked.

In unison, we replied, "No, officer. We would never do that." That had to be the least impassioned plea he had heard that day.

35

The officer reached over, patted my khaki pocket, and turned it inside out. As soon as he did, a big glob of gunpowder fell out. We were busted. For some reason, the first thought that crossed my mind was to tell the officer I didn't know how that powder got in my pocket, but I knew that would sound stupid. TC continued fake crying while my mind took in what was happening. As I peered into the back of one of the cars, there sat Dirty Red with a big grin on his face. I knew, at that moment, we were doomed. He looked like the snitch he was, and all I could think was the cops had given him a popsicle and a soda as his reward for telling on us. I should have known he couldn't be trusted.

With no confession from us, the officers threw TC and me into the back of the car where Dirty Red sat. We said nothing to him and just looked straight ahead. The officers drove us the two blocks to where Dirty Red lived and let him out without so much as a warning.

With Dirty Red free and clear, the officer turned around and looked at TC and me sitting in the back seat of the car. "You know, firecrackers are illegal. I should take you two over to juvy," he said. "Yeah, they'll make punks out of you two." That was right up my alley. In our neighborhood, anyone who went to juvenile hall came back to the 'hood with an air of glory and toughness that caused the homeboys to admire him. That was the way you got your rep built up. I wanted that.

By this time, people from all around the neighborhood had rushed outside to see what all the commotion was about. There we were, in the 'hood, with an audience of people watching us about to be hauled off to juvy. *What better way to earn some street cred?* I thought. Just then, a guy we knew as Smooth came running up to the cop car. This guy was an ex-Vietnam war hero, and word had it that he was a Black Panther. What he did next was unexpected and nothing short of miraculous. Right there in front of the whole neighborhood, Smooth got on his knees and begged that policeman not to take us away to juvy. "Listen, officer, these young men are good kids," Smooth said. Sweat was dripping down his entire face. "Turn them over to me. I'll make sure they stay on the straight and narrow." I had never seen anybody plead like that. He was begging that officer like his own life was at stake. "They won't get into any more trouble. Please, officer."

By now, all the bystanders had blocked the police car so the officer couldn't drive off. He stood there for a moment looking down at Smooth. Then, he looked around at the crowd. "All right, I'll let them go this time," he said. "But if I catch you where I think you shouldn't be, it's all over." Then, he opened the doors to let us out of the squad car. As the crowd parted, he drove away.

Smooth crumbled even further onto the sidewalk in relief. I, on the other hand, was pissed. I don't know about TC, but I was thinking, *Man, you're robbing me of my glory. What are you talking about? I could have gone to juvy! What are you doing?* I was upset with Smooth because he got us off. As crazy as it sounds, I wanted to go to juvy to earn my rep. I wanted to kick Smooth in the gut as he lay there sobbing and sweating, but I didn't. I didn't even say thank you. I just walked away. Head down and kicking rocks along the way, I started walking home.

Suddenly, out of the crowd, somebody reached from behind and sucker punched me. The fist came out of nowhere and landed straight on my left jaw like a bag of nickels. It was my grandmother. Everyone was laughing. I was stunned. She had been on her way home from the grocery store when the scene played out and had stood in the back of the crowd, watching to see what would happen. When she saw the policeman let us go, she made her way in my direction. After the punch, she grabbed the neck of my T-shirt and nearly dragged me the rest of the way home. When we got to the house, my mom went off on me. She already knew what had happened. That's how fast news travels in the 'hood. She yelled and cursed and beat me for what seemed like an hour.

Then, Dad came home. "That's enough," he said. By the tone of his voice, with those two simple words, I knew he was disappointed in me. That hurt.

I knew it would be a long time and a lot of work before I could make it up to Dad. Still, I held on to my warped desire to build up a rep so my homeboys would respect me. That is what happens when you live in darkness. You don't even understand what you are doing to yourself. You become like a misguided warrior. You might have a lot of heart, but you are operating on the wrong information. That creates chaos. When you operate out of chaos you add time and pain and struggle to your journey to find your purpose. Even that is by design because every struggle takes you one step closer to figuring out your reason for being. Take away the struggle and you take away your path to understanding your reason for living. In this sense, there are no regrets. After all, to regret is to not understand that this life is a proving ground designed to make you better.

Coming Face-to-Face with Death

If you have never been to a waistline party, you don't know what you're missing. Back in the day, people in the 'hood would have these parties at their home and invite friends from all over town. Now that I think about it, this was probably a way for the host to pocket some money to help pay rent or buy groceries for the week. Everyone would come dressed in their party clothes, and someone at the door would measure their waist to determine what they would pay to get in. The cost was a penny per inch, which did not amount to much for us teenagers.

One night, my mom and her girlfriends went out for a night of enjoyment and left us kids at home. "I don't want anybody leaving this house," she said as she grabbed her purse. "Don't even go outside on the steps, you hear me? Everybody better be here when I get back."

All of her kids fell in line with my mother's admonitions and rules, except me. Wallace, my eldest brother, was at work. My eldest sister, Michelle, decided she would keep us all entertained by putting on one of her Easy Bake Oven demonstrations. Pie was into her own world, her nose deep into whatever book she was reading at the time. The youngest kids, Valerie and Brian, were playing a board game, oblivious to the fact that they would be left home with their elder siblings in charge. However, I had an entirely different way of looking at that situation. This was not a chance at family time with my siblings; it was an opportunity to spread my wings and do my own thing. *Yeah, sure, those are your rules*, I thought, and I was willing to take whatever degree of punishment came my way as a result of where my overactive imagination led me. That night, it led me to the waistline party.

Five minutes after my mom was gone, I slipped out the back door, hopped a couple of fences, and made it to the waistline party. The problem with those kinds of parties was that they attracted people from all parts of town, and that mix was not good. Guys from the Magnolia Projects showed up because when there were young women and testosterone involved, guys tried to out dance each other to win the favor of a young maiden. There I was with a friend of mine named Gregory McGee. Greg was like a big brother to me. Everyone from young to old loved Greg because he was such a nice guy. He had impeccable manners and was respectable, charismatic, and a natural leader. He was like a Renaissance man to me because he was the first Black guy I knew of who was into the hard rock sounds of Jimi Hendricks. Greg was a good person with a good heart. Unfortunately, that led to his demise.

We had only been at the party for about an hour when a guy who lived in our neighborhood, Lenard, got into an argument with a guy from the Magnolia Projects. Lenard was a real loser. He was the neighborhood wino, liar, and coward, a fake tough guy, who regaled us with stories of things he never actually did.

All of that came to bear the night of the party. One harsh word led to another and an argument ensued. The young lady hosting the party told them to take it outside because she didn't want any fighting in her parents' house. Once they got outside, Lenard realized these guys from the projects were packing heat. Being the coward he was, Lenard coaxed Greg to stand in for him and confront those guys. Greg took his spot, and I walked out to watch my hero take care of business.

The next thing I knew, the guy from the projects walked up to Greg, yelling and ready to fight. Greg took off his shirt, ready for the scuffle, but before we knew it, this guy smacked Greg in the mouth with the tip of his .45. As soon as Greg got hit in the mouth he knew what it was, so he took off running. I froze as I bore witness to what happened next. Everything played out in slow motion, just like in the movies. I was less than five feet away from the guy with the gun. My mind was telling me to duck behind a car, but I couldn't move. In a flash, the spark shot out of the gun, and the bullet came out and hit Greg in his back. Pop, pop, pop! He was shot six times before he fell to the ground face first. I watched my friend's body jerk up and down as he gurgled for air and blood poured out of his back. Still frozen, I saw blurs of the guys from the projects whiz past me. They ran so fast I couldn't tell who was who. All I knew was my friend had just been shot and he was probably dead.

The commotion attracted a crowd from the surrounding houses, including a guy from the neighborhood, a nurse who had just gotten home from his shift at Turo hospital. He was transgender, which back then was strange, but everyone in the neighborhood accepted him because he didn't try to hide who he was. Still dressed in his white nurse's uniform, he gave Greg

CPR and tried to stop the bleeding by applying pressure to the wounds, but the blood kept pouring out. He was on the ground with my friend for less than ten minutes. When he got up his clothes were soaked with the deep red blood of Gregory McGee. I kept thinking, *Come on, Greg, get up. You can beat this.* In fact, he couldn't, and he didn't. He was dead.

I was stunned and devastated. He had gone into that party so full of life. To have the last image I saw of him be bullets tearing through his flesh and then watch him gasp for air as his blood spilled onto the ground was like watching Superman die.

What happened afterward on that sidewalk is a blur. Somehow, I made my way three blocks to my house. I don't remember getting home, but I made it. By the time I opened the front door, my mom was waiting for me. The old folks were our CNN back then, so she already knew what had happened, and she had rushed home to meet me there. I'd never seen my mom as scared as she was that night, but she was also mad. She hugged me so tight she could have broken me. Then, she hit me with the back of her hand because I had defied the rules she had set that were intended to keep me safe. Instead of that smack in the face, I needed a hug and some therapy.

As the days went on, I was in a state of shock. Losing Greg was the hardest thing I'd ever experienced. He was fearless and sensitive to others. Maybe that is what got him killed. He had so much potential. There's no telling what he could have become someday if he had been allowed to reach the fullness of who he was. But all his somedays were gone.

That experience taught me how some people devalue life. Some people who are forced to live in a low socioeconomic situation develop survival tendencies that devour the whole community and kill their own future potential and that of others, like Greg. Those guys from the projects didn't just kill a person; they killed a part of themselves. Shortly after that, those bad guys who killed Greg died mysteriously—all of them.

I have often thought about that night. If that bullet had killed me, my entire life would never have been. That experience caused me to realize I do not like conflict and confusion, so I decided the best way to avoid it was to eliminate contact with people. I became a loner and retreated into myself. From that night on, I withdrew from everyone. I didn't even go to Greg's funeral. There were times in my aloneness that I drifted off into darkness. It was easy because there was no one around to stop me.

The Misguided Warrior

By the time I reached high school, I had developed my own mind and my own way of seeing things. I thought I knew everything and could handle anything life threw at me. After losing Greg and experiencing so much pain at a young age, I was void of a valuable element of life—my childhood innocence. My withdrawal from social contact was more a protection mechanism—much like a turtle going into its shell for safety—than an escape from reality. Even my family didn't know the pain I was feeling because, during those times, you didn't talk about feelings and how crises affected you. You just went on with life. Still, one distraction after another came along to snatch all the good out of me. Actually, I let it all in, and suddenly, the bad didn't seem so bad. My consciousness became so dulled that I accepted the life I witnessed around me as the way things were supposed to be. I figured the violence and chaos were a rite of passage and it was just the way my life was going to play out. Why fight it? I saw so much talent go down the drain, and I was right there getting sucked into that nightmare.

While at Walter L. Cohen High School, I found myself adrift, going through the motions of life. I didn't realize it at the time, but sports would become a crucial lifeline for me. As with most kids who choose sports as an outlet for youthful energy, some of my biggest influencers were my coaches. Among them was Coach Audrich, our head football coach. He was similar to my father in that he was low key, had an even-keeled temperament, and was supportive and nurturing. He had a dignified demeanor, very proper and professional. He saw me as a leader, and I wanted to live up to his expectations, not for myself, but for him. He saw pro qualities in me back then, but I didn't realize he saw me that way. Beyond the football field, I really wanted to gain Coach Audrich's respect.

Another of our coaches, Coach Walker, had an equally positive impact on me. Coach Walker was young, straight out of college, with a solid, strong personality. He was smart, caring, energetic, and in many ways, he allowed me to dream. Coach Walker had a beautiful wife and a son to whom he was very attentive. One Sunday, he invited about a dozen of the leaders on the team to his home for fellowship. His wife prepared an unbelievable spread and invited us to eat our fill. He laid out the upcoming year and discussed with us our plans. That night is forever etched in my memory as one of the more positive experiences I had growing up.

When the game against Bogalusa High School in Southeast Louisiana came around, our team was ready. For kids growing up in Louisiana, Bogalusa was a forbidden place. We heard bits and pieces about its history from the elders. When we were quiet and playing the "be seen but not heard" role, we would hear them discuss some of the many atrocities that had taken place in that old lumber town. This was a place where the heroic Deacons for Defense first started. These were African American men who went off to World War II and, upon their return, armed themselves to protect the citizens in their community from being terrorized and lynched. They pre-dated the Black Panthers and put the Klan in their place. On the heels of that tradition, we felt we had something to uphold.

Our away games were the highlight of the football season because, for many of us, that was the only opportunity we had to see something other than the streets we grew up in. All the guys planned to go in like we were cool. We wanted to impress the ladies and the guys from that backwater town, so they could see we weren't a bunch of country bumpkins, like we thought they were. We were from the big city. Coach Walker, with support from Coach Audrich, wanted us to show up looking like respectable young men in shirts, ties, and blazers. I didn't like it, so I started complaining about it, not to the coaches, but to my teammates. I was supposed to be a leader on the team, but I allowed the latest fashion trends to supersede that. Looking back, I was truly a misguided warrior.

The guys were hanging out in the locker room one day after practice, and I told them all, "You know what, I'm not wearing a tie. Man, that's not my style." I went on and on about how I wanted to show up at Bogalusa High School looking fresh and how a tie would mess up my style. I wanted to show up there to be, as we used to say, ragging and pinning. I thought I sounded smart, in charge, like I was not about to let anybody tell me how to dress. What I didn't know was that Coach Audrich was within earshot. He had heard my foolish rant about something so minor, which was really meant to help us clean up, show up, and represent our community in a positive way. Instead of realizing our coaches' intent and standing in support of it, as a leader would, I chose rebellion. I decided to use my voice to influence the team in another direction. I should have been inspiring them. Instead, I nearly started a riot. The guys were fired up, screaming about how they were not about to be told how to dress. It was crazy. I felt powerful because I had gotten them to become so emotionally connected to an idea that came from me. It made me feel big.

I had fallen into a state that I discovered years later, working with young males, is the reason many of them are so easily co-opted by gangs. In a nutshell, they feel powerless. At home, they are told what to do by their mothers and, in some cases, their fathers. At school, those in authority have say-so over their behavior. For boys, feeling power and being in charge is important. They want to be connected and to have a voice. What I have learned from working with young people is that they need to be connected to and believe in something bigger than themselves.

In the midst of all the ruckus, Coach Walker stepped into the locker room and pulled me to the side. "Listen, man, I don't know what you're trying to do here, but I gotta tell you that Coach Audrich was standing outside the locker room. He heard you." I immediately felt low. It felt like someone had taken my breath away. I was embarrassed of my words and ashamed of how I had gotten the guys all riled up. "What you did was wrong, Roy. You have to repair what you damaged," he said, and then he walked away, leaving me in the hallway alone.

I turned and dropped my head in shame. All the while, the guys were still growling in the locker room about not wearing a tie. It all sounded so stupid in that moment. I had started it all and I knew what I had to do. I went into the equipment room and saw Coach Audrich. His eyes were teary. I could tell I had greatly wounded him. A grown man crouched over, sobbing. I had disappointed him that much. Really, I had disappointed myself. I was crushed.

Coach James Audrich

"Coach, I'm really sorry about what I said back there," I said. He wiped tears from his face, but didn't look at me. "I was just messing around with the guys and it got out of hand. I'll make it right. I'll go in and tell them to do what you and Coach Walker said. We need to dress in our best clothes to make a good impression. You're right. I'm sorry."

That was the first time in my life I was confronted with having to make something right that I had done. It was hard. Seeing Coach Audrich crumbled and disappointed in me was even harder. It hurt me as bad as when my dad was disappointed in me. My behavior was not only immature; it was also irresponsible and petulant, and it was a reflection of the way I viewed myself. I was hiding from the leader within who was trying to emerge. Rather than stand for something, I had chosen to resist authority. I don't even know why I did it. Was it to gain the respect of my teammates? Was it to prove my independence? Whatever the reason and whatever I thought I would gain from my behavior, it didn't satisfy me. In fact, I was ashamed of myself.

Thankfully, Coach Audrich accepted my apology. He was so proud of me for coming to him and making things right that he made redemption easy. He never held it against me. That experience showed me that I had to take responsibility for my actions and repair what I had broken. I had to understand the role I occupied and do the hard thing even when the easy thing was right there in front of me. I had to lead and be the example when everything inside of me wanted to run with the crowd, even when the crowd was wrong.

Change, however, is not easy. Despite being presented with opportunities to stand up as a leader and an individual, I fell into the crowd mentality time after time. With each instance, I went deeper into the darkness. In my senior year of high school, a guy introduced me to smoking marijuana. That's when I learned of my addictive nature. At times throughout my life, that character trait has worked for me in terms of setting goals and sticking to them, like running fourteen marathons or even writing this book. That same addictive element worked against me throughout my youth by enticing me to do things that turned out to be harmful to myself. Whenever the darkest version of this reared up, a strange, nihilistic persona would overtake me and drive me towards fatalistic behaviors, causing me to believe the lie that a life of destruction, and everything tied to it, was inevitable. It was a familiar, reliable friend. That was not how I was raised, but that life called to me. It yearned for my attention like the scab on a wound that will not heal. Like the biblical prodigal son, I had to go out and scratch the itch.

Just like the prodigal son, I had everything I needed at home—basic as it might have been—but I wanted more. I loved the vibe of the city because that was all I knew, but I needed to know what I was missing, what was outside the confines of New Orleans, with its gumbo and second line dancing and carefree lifestyle. So when my chance at a college education outside of the city came along, I jumped at it. Football had been the outlet for expressing my gift of athleticism, what I thought up to that point could be my purpose in life. I saw football as a possible ticket to something bigger. I had no idea how far it would take me, but I was ready for the ride, whether I was prepared or not. What I was not ready for was life outside of the familiar confines of my community.

THE PRODIGAL SON

The Creator designed this world to give us choices. Our job is to choose. Along every step of this journey called life, I've had options. Sometimes, those options seemed unattractive, and the choices seemed difficult to make. Other times, they were easy. Confess and go to juvy or shut up and let someone save you from yourself. Go to the party or stay home. Be the leader or use your words to incite a negative protest. These were all choices I had to make, and I made them. Best of all, they made me the person who would take the next step and the next to become who I am today. Little did I know that each choice point was a lesson, a guidepost, a test, and a proving ground for the next level of life that I would experience. I learned—albeit it on the long and rough road of hard knocks—that my ability to see the choices before me, and to make the right choice for me at every turn, is singularly reliant on me. That is a truth I had to come to as I continued life's journey.

> *Luke 15:11 And He said, "A certain man had two sons; 15:12 and the younger of them said to his father, 'Father, give me the share of the estate that falls to me.' And he divided his wealth between them. 15:13 And not many days later, the younger son gathered everything together and went on a journey into a distant country, and there he squandered his estate with loose living."*

Just like the prodigal son in biblical times, I had everything I needed to live a good life. For some reason, that didn't satisfy me. My dissatisfaction, coupled with my wanton curiosity, caused me to want something else, the bright, shiny objects of life. Wanting something else was not the problem. The real problems came when I chose to do the things I did in order to get what I wanted. In my instance, the wealth I squandered was my self-respect, the family pride that had been instilled in me as a kid, and the confidence I had built up through discovering my athletic ability.

To get back to myself and get on track with who the Creator intended me to be, I had to wake up, but waking up was not easy. I had to struggle within and even struggle without. As I did, I slowly and silently realized that my situation was of my own making and every choice I made was mine alone. Choosing the right direction for myself was a struggle each time because there were always so many options, the least of which was doing nothing at all and remaining in the low place.

> *Luke 15:14 "Now, when he had spent everything, a severe famine occurred in that country, and he began to be in need. 15:15 And he went and attached himself to one of the citizens of that country, and he sent him into his fields to feed swine. 15:16 And he was longing to fill his stomach with the pods that the swine were eating, and no one was giving anything to him."*

Waking up and choosing to get back to myself—my true self—was the most liberating part of the journey. It involved a pilgrimage into self-realization and admitting to myself where I had gone wrong. Many times, I wanted to blame someone else for my state. I wanted someone to throw me some crutches, to open my head and pour knowledge in to help me along the way, but the world doesn't work that way. One of the most powerful things in life is free will. Life was teaching me self-reliance, self-respect, and responsibility, not helplessness and dependency. The struggles I faced, both internal and external, were of my making and they were my responsibility to face and to overcome. As hard as it was, I had to do it. During each critical step, I had to clean up, to remove myself from the mess I had created and build something new, from the inside out. It was humbling and at times embarrassing. What I have come to know is that cleaning up is not one and done; it's perpetual.

> ***Luke 15:17*** *"But when he came to his senses, he said, 'How many of my father's hired men have more than enough bread, but I am dying here with hunger!* ***15:18*** *I will get up and go to my father, and will say to him, "Father, I have sinned against heaven, and in your sight;* ***15:19*** *I am no longer worthy to be called your son; make me as one of your hired men."'"*

As a product of the public school system, I learned early on that no one is going to do the work for me that I should do for myself. Not even the Creator works in my favor unless I activate Him by putting forward effort. Faith without action does not work. So when I put forth the effort, the Creator moves in my life in a supernatural way. I've experienced this more times than I can count. Activating that supernatural support system is all about standing up.

> ***Luke 15:20*** *"And he got up and came to his father. But while he was still a long way off, his father saw him and felt compassion for him, and he ran and embraced him, and kissed him.* ***15:21*** *And the son*

said to him, 'Father, I have sinned against heaven and in your sight; I am no longer worthy to be called your son.' **15:22** *But the father said to his slaves, 'Quickly bring out the best robe and put it on him, and put a ring on his hand and sandals on his feet;* **15:23** *and bring the fattened calf and kill it, let us eat and be merry.* **15:24** *for this son of mine was dead and has come to life again; he was lost, and has been found.' And they began to be merry."*

When I first heard the concept of "wake up, clean up, and stand up," it went through me like a hot knife through butter. I heard it in a speech given by Dr. Malauna Karenga, the originator of the celebration of Kwanzaa, and he referenced Malcolm X as the source of this tri-part journey. It was manna from heaven for me. All the floodlights turned on inside my spirit, and I have been processing the concept ever since. As I returned to this life-altering theory, I added a final step that exemplifies the bold action made possible only once the first three steps are complete—show up.

The rationale for why one should wake up is that if you don't, you will never be able to see clearly what is around you and before you. The state in which you exist might have been influenced by outside forces, but your own choices and actions have led you there. Waking up is one thing, but it can be dangerous if you're not ready to do something about it. You could sink further into your misery. Having the fortitude to wake up to your current state and open your eyes to see the truth of your life is a game-changing experience.

Once awake, you must clean up. This is where the real effort begins, the hard part, and it is ongoing. To clean up, you have to unpack the old baggage and remove the burdens of your past so you can more easily move into what's next in your life. Free from the burdens of the past, you have to stand up for yourself and your values. Finally, you're ready to show up for yourself, your family, and your community. That is the journey of life we all go through if we are willing to endure it.

Wake Up

Luke 15:17"But when he came to his senses, he said, 'How many of my father's hired men have more than enough bread, but I am dying here with hunger! 15:18 I will get up and go to my father, and will say to him, "Father, I have sinned against heaven, and in your sight; 15:19 I am no longer worthy to be called your son; make me as one of your hired men."""

I could not have found my true self in the uptown New Orleans community I grew up in. I needed to leave the familiar in order to experience the fullness of myself and my abilities. I had to isolate myself in an unfamiliar place. I was among the first generation of my family to go to college, and I was recruited by dozens of colleges, among them Tulane University in New Orleans.

Wealthy people were courting me, and at one event after another, I was handed white envelopes stuffed with money as an enticement to attend different local universities. Tulane was one of them. That was the way things worked back then, so I decided to game the system. I was dead set on going to Tulane for all the wrong reasons. In my warped mind, I would extract as much money as I could to further my nefarious activity in my hometown, with no concern about my academic pursuits or what was best for me. Tulane would be an excellent cover. After all, I knew the ins and outs of the city, and as a football star, I could really do some damage. I was ready to get to Tulane to hustle, get over, get by, and get as much money as I could. I figured if they were crazy enough to let me in the school, they deserved whatever happened. As fate would have it, a college career at Tulane was not in my future.

At the end of the football season, coach Benny Ellington, who had been recruiting me to attend Tulane, was let go. The new coach brought in his regime, and suddenly, I was on the outside looking in. I visualized my college dreams dashed and I began to panic. I didn't know what to do next. Thankfully, Coach Audrich took over and guided me to a safe landing. He sent letters to a bunch of schools on my behalf, but my heart was set on attending an HBCU. I don't know why. Maybe I thought I would be safer there, less likely to get lost among a sea of people who did not look like me and did not give a damn about my future. Maybe I didn't want to be the token on the team or in the classroom because I wouldn't know how to be in that environment. By then, I was happy to take just about any offer that took me out of state and allowed me a full ride.

Alcorn State University was that place for me. Even though I had my share of academic slip-ups, I managed to maintain the grades to get into college, unlike other athletes who slid in on a wing and a prayer. Once accepted at Alcorn in 1976, I was relieved. Still, I didn't feel prepared for what lay ahead. My college experience was what I needed to detox, but little did I know it would bring new and interesting diversions.

Not long after I left home, I started to feel disenchanted about where I came from. New Orleans had become "less than," a myth, a fabricated place others viewed as all fun and frolic, but which I recalled with a sour taste in my mouth. Up to that point, I thought New Orleans was the center of the world. I still loved the city. It had a hold on my heart, but I could see the warts, the lack, the dull finish. I loved my family and missed them, but I remembered the pain of growing up in the 'hood and that remained foremost in my mind whenever I thought about home. Still, I held on to some great memories, like training with my buddies in Shakespeare Park, where we ran the track every day in the noonday heat. Off to the side, the winos and gamblers would sit in the bleachers, betting on which one of us would cross the finish line first. I always did. That was a metaphor for my life in New Orleans. Me running hard, someone else betting on the outcome, usually against me, no one realizing the potential we all had for a better life.

When I left New Orleans, I didn't realize that I was totally unprepared for college, academically and athletically. Still, going away to college was a pivotal point in my life, just not in the way it is for most people. Many families prepare their kids for the college experience. Parents plan for years to take their kid off to college. They talk about their expectations for how they should behave. They buy all the things the kids will need in their dorm room, pack up their stuff, and drive to the campus together. It's a ritual for most, but it wasn't for me. I didn't have all those things. There was no checklist, no guidelines, no insight into what I should have or expect. My motto was "Not having is no reason for not getting," so my buddies and I worked and hustled to pull together what we thought we would need once we arrived on campus. The shame of being unprepared caused me to retreat further into myself emotionally and to cover up my discomfort with behaviors that didn't support my well-being.

By the time I arrived at college, I had become a knucklehead. I was doing drugs and selling drugs and slipping into a life where I was dead to myself and everybody around me. That new life was fun at first, but I knew I wasn't raised like that, and I knew it would not last. I wanted more for myself than the street life that had consumed so many of my childhood friends. I began to look for something more, something better.

The town where I ended up in college, Lorman, Mississippi, was a far cry from anything sophisticated. It couldn't hold a candle to the vibe and energy of my hometown. Even still, I became mesmerized by all the new people and experiences there and in the nearby town of Port Gibson, with its one Piggly Wiggly market and one streetlight. I was introduced to people who were different and had the potential to enrich my life. All of that made me less rigid in my thinking. Those new things tickled my fancy and titillated my appetites. It was like an addiction grabbing hold of me. Initially, I was a bystander, just watching. In time, I could not resist the pull, the attraction of the newness right before me. As with anything, I had to be careful what I introduced into my life early on because I didn't want to spend a lifetime chasing it out.

My first year at Alcorn State University was a blur. I was not ready for the academic rigor or the structure. I was not organized. I didn't know how to pick classes. I didn't know how to study. I had no idea what was before me. I went up there with my homeboys, and all we were interested in was playing football and creating mayhem. I didn't have a clue what I was doing. I was not ready mentally, emotionally, or spiritually for college life. I wasn't ready to leave home, even though I wanted to.

My first night on campus, my roommate had not arrived, so I was in the dorm room by myself. The moment I got in that room and closed the door, I cried. I cried because I was alone. I cried because of my fear of what would happen next. I cried because I didn't know what the heck I had gotten into. I had experienced a lot of traumatic things growing up, from overcoming tuberculosis to seeing someone get killed right in front of me, but I had never experienced anything that so dramatically interrupted my way of being as living on a strange campus amid strangers who knew nothing about me. I craved the rambunctious activity of my siblings, the reassuring words of my mom and dad, and the calmness of my Uncle Nick. I was alone and afraid. The shock and the culture overwhelmed me. So that night, I cried.

Having ended my secondary education on a wing and a prayer, I wasn't successful in the classroom my first year at Alcorn. I didn't know how to structure my schedule to have the proper time to study, so my days were one blur after another. It was like being in the vortex of a tornado. To hide my confusion and discomfort, I wore these dark glasses everywhere I went on campus. I didn't say much because I didn't know what to say. I was afraid that, as soon as I spoke, my cover would be blown; they would know I was a fraud because I had no real substance.

I didn't have many friends, other than my boys who had come to Alcorn with me. The other students perceived me as a cool guy, but really, I was insecure and scared. I hid behind my persona as the mysterious guy from New Orleans. When I was with my friends, the party always happened around us. I took that very slim sliver of a thing and played it to the max, but there was no substance behind it. If my off-the-field life was a confused mess, my on-the-field perspective was just as bad.

For the first time since I had started playing football as a kid, I felt out of place on the field. Without the proper mindset and guidance, I couldn't be my best, and the coaches expected everyone to be exceptional on the field. Each pre-camp practice included full-equipment, full-contact participation three times a day. Once school started, we went to twice daily practices that were equally intense. It felt like a military bootcamp in that it was all designed to manipulate your mind. It definitely wasn't for the faint of heart. That kind of taxing activity, day after day, puts a lot of pressure on the body and the mind.

The mental part was far worse than the physical. Each guy on the field had been recruited and promised all sorts of things, like a starting position, becoming an All-American, and even a place in the NFL. From my viewpoint, the recruiters did not do their jobs well. Instead of scouting for mental and emotional acumen, they looked for guys who could run fast, tackle hard, kick far, and perform on the field. There seemed to be no requirement that we also have the mental fortitude to think through challenges, make decisions that would serve us and the team, or withstand the multitude of pressures that come with being a student athlete. As a result, so many guys fell off. They dropped like flies, either on the field from exhaustion or off the field because they didn't go to class. As hard as it all was, the thought of quitting left me feeling more like a massive failure than I felt struggling to figure it all out, so I decided to stick it out and give it my all. I would either rise to the top or kill myself trying.

On the field, I created my fame. I turned my fear into aggression and became out of control, like a junkyard dog, mean and nasty. One day, the coach called me out and he put me one-on-one with my roommate, Earnest Young, who was All-American. Earnest was smaller than I was, and there was something the coach wanted him to do that he wasn't doing well. So the coach decided to pit my brute force against his. By this time, the coach had started calling me his attack dog, his pit bull, because of my blind fierceness.

"Get in the ring, Young," he shouted to me. "Get in there with Young!"

They put us in what was called the bullring, where guys would attack each other like two rams. Whoever ended up on his back was the loser. It became a match of Young against Young. The other guys gathered around us like we were in a wrestling match. The coach lifted his hands, and when he dropped them, we attacked each other.

I ran Earnest over, knocked him down, and knocked him out. From there, the legend was born on the field, just like on the playground when I was eleven years old. I had a glimmer of hope that, just maybe, I belonged there after all. With that single incident, I had earned my credibility on the field, and that boosted my confidence off the field. I wasn't a better student, but I felt like I could hold my head up as I walked across campus. The dark shades I wore became less of a disguise and more of a prop, part of the costume I wore as a self-defined badass athlete. Still, I had no substance. My self-worth was tied up in my image as an athlete. Some days I loved it; some days I didn't. For the most part, that quasi-celebrity status got me the attention I wanted from the campus groupies. As with most things in life, I didn't realize what I was missing until it walked across campus right in front of me. When I saw what I saw, I was smitten.

The time between classes was hang-out time for me. My buddies and I had a spot on campus where we would gather and shoot the breeze. We really should've been studying or doing something constructive, but we wanted to be seen. Most days, we paid no attention to the other students walking past, but this particular day, someone caught my eye. When I saw Kathleen Crawford walk across campus, I froze. I was hypnotized by her grace and the way she held her head up. She was wearing a business power look—a nicely fitted dress with a pretty black jacket and black heels—and she was carrying a black leather briefcase. She looked like she was on a mission. I had to know her. I told my friends I would catch up with them later, and then I ran up behind Kathleen as she walked into one of the buildings on campus. I reached the door just as she did, and I opened it for her.

My future wife, Kathleen Crawford

"Hey, pretty lady, how are you?" I asked in the smoothest voice I could muster. She looked at me suspiciously, then smiled courteously and kept walking. "Hey, what's your name, baby?" I said in my mack voice, shuffling behind her like a puppy.

Still walking at her normal pace, she said, "Kathleen, and I'm busy. I have some studying to do. I don't have time for your silliness."

Undeterred, I followed her up the stairs, down a hallway, and into a room with rows of books, still talking and trying to get her to slow down and look at me. Nothing I said worked. "Listen, I'm not trying to hurt you, I just wanna talk, li'l mama," was my desperate plea.

Then I heard a chorus of "Shhhhh!" ripple through the room. Kathleen selected a table and placed her briefcase down. I didn't even realize she was dropping a hint by choosing a table with only a single chair.

"Listen, let me just have your number, and I'll call you later," I begged.

"Shhhhh!" came the sounds again.

I looked around the room for the shushers and said, "Hey, don't be shushing me! I'm trying to get me a girlfriend, here!"

Then, Kathleen looked up at me and whispered, "Are you crazy, you fool? You're in the library. You need to be quiet." She was clearly embarrassed. "Please leave me alone," she said.

That's how I found out the school had a library. I hadn't known it was there, but after that, I frequented the library, hoping I would see her again. I did see her several times, but I just watched her from a distance. I noticed how she organized her books and notebooks, how she flipped through the pages of books and took notes. Unbeknownst to her, she was demonstrating to me how to study.

This was my first semester, and I had an incomplete in just about every class because I never attended and wasn't participating. That landed me on academic probation and then in summer school to repair my grades and get me up to speed for my sophomore year. I had no clue how to be successful in college. I was a failure academically, but a success on the field and around campus. Brushing aside my poor grades, I felt like I was on top, until I hit rock bottom.

My transformation from a quiet, low-key freshman to a wild and out-of-control jock was sudden and undeniable. I was cocky, not because I was sure of myself, but because I was scared I would be exposed for the fraud I felt lived inside me. I was confused, and I had a lot of anger because I felt the adults in my life hadn't prepared me for this reality that offered a promise which seemed just out of reach. The reality was it wasn't them; it was me and my rebellious spirit that led me to this point. Thank God I had sports as an outlet to express my aggression. Without that, I probably would've been in prison or dead. Little did I know I needed a strong figure to grab my attention, someone who could see deep inside me, beyond the façade. Coach Marino Casem was that savior.

One of the most legendary figures in athletics, Coach Marino Casem stands shoulder-to-shoulder with greats among historically Black colleges and within the entirety of college football, coaches like Eddie Robinson and Paul "Bear" Bryant. Much of the success and equity that smaller schools experience today is due in large part to the work Coach Casem and others did to voice the unique concerns of HBCUs. Throughout his career, he led a lot of the battles that admitted young people into major universities. In fact, he is the reason many historically black institutions still exist today. He was a life force, a combination of Martin Luther King, Malcolm X, Muhammad Ali, and Richard Pryor, all wrapped into one incredible man. I had never met a man like him. I believe God put him in my life to arrest my thinking and to set me on the path I needed to travel to become the best version of myself.

During those days, a party wasn't a party until I showed up with my boys. One night, I talked my way into a party hosted by a bunch of seniors in their dorm room. Some professional ladies of the night had come to town from Chicago, and there was lots of drinking and smoking going on. It was a wild scene in that dorm room. We were partying hard, and the music was blaring. Out of nowhere, Coach Butch Jones, who was over the athletic dorm, came in. The music stopped, people scattered to all corners of the room, and everyone got quiet. Parties weren't a problem, but alcohol and marijuana certainly were. Those were big no-nos for anyone who intended to remain on the team and start in any upcoming games. So there was a lot at stake, and we all knew we had just blown it.

Immediately, those seniors began to beg and grovel. They were crying like babies and asking the coach not to hold this against them. I, on the other hand, was young and too stupid to know the severity of the consequences before me. As seniors, they had a lot to lose. I was just a freshman. Already, I had established a reputation as a badass, so I was not about to let the guys or the coach see me begging. I figured I was unstoppable on the field, and with my behavior, I almost dared the coach to kick me off the team. I wasn't fazed by the threat of expulsion or probation. I was immune to the consequences of my actions, not because there were none but because I was clueless and irresponsible. Instead of begging like the others, I crossed my legs, raised my cup of cheap wine, and said, "Here's to all of you!"

The coach walked over to me and shouted, "Young, what is wrong with you? Do you want to get kicked off the team?"

I said, "Coach, unlike these guys on their knees, I admit it, you caught me. I'm busted." I figured admitting my wrongdoing was more honorable than groveling. "I'm not about to beg, Coach.

Do what you gotta do." That behavior put my entire future on the line, but I was too stupid to realize it. I thought I was being cool.

The day following the party, I questioned my actions and wondered about my fate. I worked out two scenarios: one, I would be kicked off the team and sent home, which was fine because I was homesick anyway; or two, I would be used as an example by the coach and he would assign me a hell of a lot of drills—hard work, but it would only make me stronger and improve my rep. Two days later, we were all called to Coach Casem's office to explain ourselves and learn our fate. Honestly, I figured this was my last hoorah, that I was about to be put out to pasture and sent home to New Orleans, so I dressed for a funeral. From head to toe, I was in black, including my dark shades. I figured if this was my judgment day and if I was going down, I would go down looking cool.

As I sat in the hallway with the others outside Coach's office, I heard the *pop, pop, pop* of his paddle smacking against the backside of one player after the other. They entered and exited within five minutes, emerging with a look of terror and pain on their faces. No one said a word, but their teary eyes spoke volumes.

"Where's that son-of-a-bitch Young?" I heard Coach yell from inside his office.

Just then, someone poked their head out of the office and motioned for me to enter. When I went in, Coach looked tired. He was sweating. I guess all that paddling had taken a toll on him. Still, I braced for mine.

"Take those damn glasses off," he yelled. Then, he walked around his desk and sat down. I remained standing and removed my shades. "What are you doing in my office? What is wrong with you, Young?"

I knew what he meant. He had watched my rapid rise to popularity and my transition from timid to tumultuous. Obviously, he didn't care for my new persona because it was causing him to spend time correcting things with bad actors like me when he should have been coaching the entire team.

All I could think to say was a line from a song by The Meters: "Coach, the world is a bit under the weather, and I'm not feeling too good myself."

That just pissed him off more. He called the other coaches into the office and told them what I had just said. Their faces looked as confused as his had. They had no idea what I was talking about, but I now had an audience for my paddling and that did not sit well with me.

"Put your hands on the desk," he said, staring at me as he rounded the desk to get closer. I cut my eyes at him. He yelled again, and I got the sense that I should obey. With one hand on the desk, I glanced behind me to let him know I was ready. What he did next was nothing short of a miracle. He raised that paddle so high in the air I was sure the momentum of that wood hitting my backside would split the skin under my clothes. Instead, the paddle landed gently on my rear. Just a touch, nothing more.

He said, "Do we have an understanding here, Young?" I had not yet exhaled, so I couldn't even answer. "Get out of my office. I don't want to hear any more about this kind of behavior from you."

In some ways, that gesture hurt me more than an actual lick. It reminded me of when my father would show his disappointment in me. I wanted to cry. Coach Casem had shown me mercy for no reason at all. That confused me, but it also showed me that, despite myself, someone thought I deserved a break. I left the office and walked past the others seated in the hallway. The looks on their faces questioned how I was able to survive what they knew was in store for them and still walk out of there dry-eyed and standing upright.

Legendary Coach Marino Casem

Those seniors thought I had swag. Coach Casem, on the other hand, knew I was scared and out of control. He understood that I was a confused, angry, young Black man. Rather than meet that with corporal punishment, he let me off the hook. He also demonstrated to me his disappointment in my behavior, and he did it with love, not anger. That mattered more than anything to me. Just like the rotten feeling I got each time I disappointed my dad when I was young, I never wanted to feel that way towards Coach Casem again. Coach represented many things to different people—from harsh taskmaster to charismatic, compassionate, servant-leader—but from that moment on, he was my hero, and I worked harder than ever to prove my appreciation for him.

Spiritual Awakening

Waking up is as essential as breathing air. ~Roynell Young

The biblical story says that the prodigal son came to himself, suggesting that when he left home, he was not himself. He was caught up in pride and ego and the distractions of life. His reality had to fall apart in order to arrest his thinking. That is when he realized he was at the bottom, eating what the pigs ate. He had to wake up and realize his daddy had everything the son needed and he had been too stubborn to see or appreciate it. He blew his inheritance on wine, women, and song. That's when he came to himself. The key was he humbled himself to clean up and return home. Before he could complete his speech explaining to his father how sorry he was, his father ran out, kissed him, and threw him the biggest feast because he was so happy his son had returned.

Just like the wayward son in the Bible story, the lifestyle I had adopted was totally opposite from the way I was raised. Those behaviors later became a source of shame and guilt for me. I was like a skunk. People fear skunks, not because skunks are big and scary, but because no one wants to be sprayed with their stink. Just like the prodigal son, my choices eventually led me to a place where I was metaphorically in the pig pen eating with the pigs. From wild partying to the drugs and the rebellious attitude, I had lost myself at a young age.

Then, suddenly, I snapped out of it. I literally woke up and realized "I didn't come from this." I don't know what I was thinking or why I thought that life was so great, but when I stopped to focus on the reality of what I was becoming, it brought me to tears. I felt helpless to the point that I cried out, "Lord, I don't know how to get out of what I have accidentally walked into." That life was no accident, however. I had chosen it, and I had to decide to choose something else if I wanted to become my best self. That is when I started to come back to myself, just like the prodigal son.

My parents had taught me what was right, but I had chosen something different. My prodigal-son experience was an internal challenge that forced me to leave what I intrinsically knew was me to try to be something else in the world. In that moment, I had to admit that the back-and-forth battle between doing good and dipping into various temptations actually gave substance to living for me. Those struggles made it possible to begin the journey to find myself. The bright, shiny objects had lost their luster, and I realized they were not as beneficial to me as I thought they were. I had reached the end of myself and I knew I had to rediscover my true identity. Finally, I was ready to return home, not physically but spiritually. My coming-home experience was as drastic as my leaving-home experience had been. That addictive personality reared its head again; only this time, it was in the form of a spiritual awakening. As it turned out, the home I was ready to come back to was my true self.

In 1977, one individual, whom I held in high regard, proved to be a pivotal, unsung hero in my life, my high school friend and teammate, Kemp Johnson. We had crossed paths earlier in my life, but had lost contact for a few years. In New Orleans, he was a man of the streets, and that gave him great status. In high school, he got into athletics. He had always been a good athlete, but he had spent his early years in juvenile facilities. Because of that, he didn't get to experience the full expression of himself. Kemp and I had a few run-ins over the years, but nothing serious. Despite that, we became best friends in high school.

Years later, in my sophomore year at Alcorn, my mind was focused on partying and young women. I was having a great time in this new environment where I could be whoever I wanted to be. Kemp and a few other guys had followed me to Alcorn. He was a resourceful fellow, something he learned during his time in juvy. Kemp didn't have transcripts or a scholarship, but using his street knowledge, he gamed the system for a year and a half before he was found out. He even had a work-study job in the administration building, which gave him access to his records so he could manipulate them. Soon enough, however, the system caught up with him and he was kicked out of school. He had nowhere to live and no money to stay in school, so he had to return to New Orleans.

I was upset that the school would do that to him, and I was hurt knowing I would be losing my friend. In my blind and foolish fury, I decided to protest and leave school too. It was a childish decision made in the heat of emotion. Most people would have loved that someone would be willing to throw away their own future to protest something that impacted them. As they say, "Misery loves company." It's a boost to the ego to have someone give up so much for you. But not Kemp. He grabbed me by the collar, pulled me aside, and said, "Man, whatever you do, don't leave. You have something special, and it needs to be exploited." If I didn't know better, I would have thought Kemp was about to cry right there. "You're special," he said. "You just don't see it yet. Stay. I know it's painful. I'm gonna be all right." I had a big lump in my throat because I could feel the emotion of what he said, and I knew it would be hard seeing my friend leave.

During Christmas break that year, I met up with Kemp when I went home to New Orleans. Lo and behold, he was talking and acting differently, using terms I'd heard in church growing up, but had never heard from a young person. As it turned out, he had found himself. He had found someone new. He had found Christ. Many people hear religious sermons that go in one ear and out the other because it's all noise. Much of what we call traditional religion is just showmanship, so God does not break through. Not until he shouts to us through our pain, our loss, and our grief do we hear him. Only then do we realize we are not our own gods and we have a need for something greater.

With my best friend, Kemp Johnson

I had no interest in what I perceived at that time as becoming some religious nut or a holy roller, so I tried to keep my distance from Kemp without being too obvious. One night, however, he invited me to attend an event. I could tell he knew I'd been avoiding him, and I felt guilty about it, so I agreed to go to with him. Little did I know, the event was a church revival. Had I known this in advance, I would not have gone, and he knew it. Once I was in there, and the doors were closed, I was trapped. I didn't leave, but I decided that would never happen again.

Two nights later, I stumbled home from a party around one o'clock in the morning after indulging in some adult libations. Kemp and two other guys were sitting on my front porch. They were pretty cool, but I was suspicious of their intentions because nobody just happens to be sitting on your doorstep at one o'clock in the morning. We got into a heated debate. In fact, I was prepared to get physical because they had violated my space. I hadn't invited them there. They started talking all this religious mumbo jumbo about God having a plan for me. I was in pain, so the last thing I wanted to do was hear from those guys.

One guy, Elroy Glover, was skilled in the art of debate. He finally boxed me in and talked about time, purpose, and God's plan. He impressed upon me that all of us are living on borrowed time. I listened to him and, as a result, did something counter to what I wanted to do. I took him up on his offer to accept Christ into my life. I didn't get to that point merely because they had confronted me. That decision was the result of a convergence of a number of variables that closed in on me at that moment.

I was cornered and I had to face some realities that, up to that point, I had been able to evade. I was totally caught off guard and my response was an override against my will. C.S. Lewis said, "God whispers to us in our pleasures, speaks in our conscience, and shouts in our pains." That night was a perfect orchestration of circumstances that finally allowed me to hear the Creator shouting to me. He had probably whispered before, but I had enough pleasure or distractions in my life to drown it out. Throughout my upbringing, he had spoken to me in my subconscious, but it was not enough to stop me from engaging in self-destructive behaviors. I always figured I would get around to moving closer to God at some point. But that night, I felt the pain of having no direction in my life, the sting of realizing how pointless my existence was. Kemp and his friends painted me into a corner, and I submitted.

My plan was to hear them out, blow them off, and continue what I was doing. I did not want to hear their religious talk. I had grown up in the church, so I knew all the jargon and the tradition. I had been baptized, dunked in the water, and celebrated afterward with a big party and lots of food. That was what I knew about salvation. I expected to run up against what I was familiar with so I could quickly dismiss it and move on. But to my surprise, those guys didn't give me any of that. Instead, they spoke directly to my pain, and I wasn't prepared for it. They basically said, "I want to introduce you to your Creator. This is the one who made you." That blew my mind. They explained to me that the Bible is an owner's manual to instruct me in how to live. That threw me off, and I had no way of stopping what was happening to me.

These guys were introducing me to something beyond the religion of my childhood. Religion, as I learned, is for people who are trying to avoid going to hell. Spirituality is for people who have already experienced hell on earth and who yearn for something better. That night, I was spiritually reattached to the one who made me, and it had a physical effect on me. I felt like I'd had an out-of-body experience. A part of me wanted to stop it because I didn't want to give up the life I was living, but I couldn't resist it, so I submitted.

> *The two most important days in a human being's life are the day they are born and the day they realize why they were born.*
> ~Mark Twain

A few days later, I snapped out of whatever state I had been in that night. I tried to get a redo on my life. I went back to the same party house I'd gone to days earlier, but something was different. Even though I was partaking in the same things, I could not get the same enjoyment. I felt lifeless and uncomfortable inside myself amid all the noise surrounding me. It was like a movie scene being played out, and I was an observer. A conflict had been created inside me, and I could not zone out. Something was awaking within me and it confused me.

I knew then that I could no longer use drugs as a distraction. I realized, at that moment, that my life had been a drama in which I was the main character. I had engaged in all the pleasures available to me and allowed them to distract me just enough to avoid doing what I knew was right. Everyone else in my drama made up my cast of extras. They were all a reflection of me. I had to decide, once and for all, which version of myself I wanted to hold on to, which one offered the most promise, the most life. I knew then that my decision would direct the trajectory of my future.

Slowly, Kemp and his friends coaxed me into going to Bible study, which is where I began to learn about a God I never really knew. I began to grow in that regard, but I was torn between this newfound grace and my old life. Every now and then, I would go to my old hangout, and each time, something died within me. Eventually, the word got out that I had lost my mind and fallen into that religious junk.

The game with those guys was to see how long it would take to get me high. One night, I showed up with my religious tracts in one hand and my Bible in the other. When I got there, there were about a dozen guys in the front room.

"Hey guys, let me tell you about the goodness of God," I said, all proud and jolly. I tried to use the approach Kemp and his friends had taught me. When I got no response from the audience in the room, I tried the one-on-one approach. I slid over on the sofa next to one guy and quietly said, "Hey man, you ever thought about dying?"

He looked over at me real slow and said, "Yeah, man. We're all gonna die." Then he took a long, slow drag on his joint and passed it over to me. "Here, take this."

I didn't want the joint. I wanted to get those guys to wake up and see what I had seen. With each attempt, I got no takers. Then, little by little, they began to tip-toe out. Suddenly, I was alone in the room. They had all left to get high in the other room. That night, I walked out of that house with a big, goofy smile on my face. "Well, I guess I won," I said. And I never went back.

Back at Alcorn, things weren't going well for me in school. It was rough going on the field. Being away from home hit me hard again and I felt alone. My best friend had been sent home, and I found it hard to form new relationships and friendships. Prior to going to Alcorn, the only time I had left the four-block area of uptown New Orleans that I grew up in was for away football games or to visit my grandmother in Thibodaux. Even after two years at Alcorn, I continued to feel as if I was in unfamiliar territory. As a result, I wasn't confident. This was not the active urban setting I had grown up in. It was a slow, rural existence, where I was surrounded by people and cultures totally different from my own. With the familiar safety mechanisms of home taken away from me, a lot of things converged to create a perfect situation for my encounter with Christ. Although I had accepted Christ while in New Orleans, it took me being removed from my hometown for everything in my life to stop. Once that reality hit me, I was forced to think about why I was created.

What happened to me in 1977 was a necessary part of my journey. I went from being involved in all kinds of illicit activity on campus to being a spiritual guy. God had put the world on pause, and I could no longer run from myself. I had to face me. Little did I know, that was exactly what I needed.

I credit Kemp Johnson for causing the tipping point that ushered in the new me and allowed me to become more at peace with myself and with everything around me. Although the circumstances were the same, my perspective on how to deal with them had changed. I went from a "glass half empty" person to "glass half full." I knew I was on the right path because when others who were on the dark side of life saw me coming, they would all scatter and avoid me. Before, they couldn't wait to ambush and tempt me, but something radical had happened to me. It was peculiar. Some of the people closest to me were concerned that I was having a mental breakdown. Who goes from being a nighthawk—a self-indulgent, self-centered creature of the underbelly—to being someone who sees himself as a servant wanting to help others? It alarmed my family too. They were happy for me, but they thought I had taken it too far.

During summer break after my sophomore year, I was home in New Orleans visiting my family and hanging out. Kemp and I were cruising down Canal Street in my beautiful 1976 four-door, burnt-orange Ford LTD with the JBL stereo system playing some George Benson. I might have been spiritual, but I still had some swagger. I had a Bible and some religious tracts in my hand, ready to pass out to any unsuspecting soul who happened to make eye contact with me. Off to my right, who did I see walking down the street but Coach Casem himself. "Hey, that's Coach Marino Casem!" I screamed. He was there with Mrs. Casem and defensive coordinator Dennis Thomas for the Southwestern Athletic Conference taking place in New Orleans.

I pulled over and hopped out of the car. "Hey, Coach Casem, good to see you. How are you doing? What are you doing in New Orleans?" I fired off all these questions and didn't give him a chance to answer before I proceeded to whip out my religious tracts and tell them about the goodness of God. I could tell he was shocked to see me, not only because of the energy I was putting out, but also because the last time he saw me I had a big "Jackson Five" afro. That day, my afro was gone, and I was sporting a fresh, low cut. The look on his face let me know he was leery, but I kept talking anyway. I was basically threatening him within an inch of his life to accept Christ or else he was going to hell. I was like a machine gun, spewing out words so fast that I didn't come up for air.

They were pinned against the wall on Canal Street, probably thinking, "When is this guy going to shut up?" Finally, I stopped talking, handed them each a religious tract, and wished them well during their stay in my hometown. They walked away, looking stunned, unable to say much except, "Thanks, see you later." I bet they went for a strong drink after that encounter. I had never seen Coach Casem speechless, but that encounter left him with no response.

In the decades since that fateful day, whenever I go home to visit New Orleans, while driving down Canal Street I see the religious guys—well-meaning, but so clueless—with their bullhorns, calling out to people to get saved or go to hell. They tug on someone's elbow and say, "I don't know you, but let me tell you about Jesus." I have to laugh because their hearts are in the right place, but their execution is all wrong, just like mine was back then. I've learned over time that you win the person and then you prove your point. You do not go in unannounced and invade somebody's space. I was that guy.

My religious zeal had turned into another extreme for me. I'm sure it was quite comical to onlookers. I had been living in the guilt of my past and I thought I had to make up for lost time. In my mind, I was trying to make God look good because I had sure made him look bad before. The zeal I exhibited through my spiritual conversion matched that of my previous wild life. I was violating other people's space without permission. I thought I had a point to prove, but I had not asked anyone's permission to share my passion.

When I returned to Alcorn the following fall semester, the first thing Coach Casem did was try to test me. He asked me to lead a pre-practice prayer. I could tell he was thinking I wasn't for real, like he wanted to put my religiosity to the test. My first thought was *No way! Don't put that on me. I'm no preacher. I've got a lot of growing in front of me.* I wasn't ready to pray in public, but I gave it my best. I remembered how hyped I'd been when I saw him in New Orleans, and I knew I had to deliver, so I gave it my all.

When I finished the prayer, I intentionally avoided his gaze. I did not want the expression on his face to give me any signals about his approval or disapproval of the prayer. I had dug deep down in my spirit to share the word of God with my teammates, and I wanted that to be enough for me. At that moment, I did not need Coach's approval, and that felt good.

During the remainder of my college years, I became a spiritual leader and a positive example for others on campus. Guys started coming to my room for hangout sessions, basically informal Bible studies. We would talk about their challenges and what was happening in their lives. Talking with them was so natural for me, but I had no idea what I was providing for them. It was something all the men in my life had done for me. For some of those guys, I came to learn, it made a world of difference.

As time went on, I took the path of trying to figure out my purpose in life through my Creator. By the time my junior year rolled around, I could sense the growth in myself, and obviously Coach Casem saw it too. That was the year his father passed away. Of all the people he could have turned to seeking understanding about it, he turned to me. He wanted to know what death and dying were all about and how God played into it. In short, he was looking to discover what God was trying to say to him. His trust in me was a sacred honor and, in a way, that conversation redefined our relationship.

Every time I saw him after that, we would laugh about that day on Canal Street. He told me years later that he went back to Alcorn and told the staff, "God dammit! I lost the best defensive back I ever had at this school. Young has turned into a religious nut! Now he's not going to want to hit anybody; he's gonna be soft. Man, why did he have to get poisoned with this religion?" Of course, it was no surprise to me to hear him say that. I knew I had gone over the deep end in those early years of my spiritual awakening. Thankfully, I eventually progressed from religion to spirituality, from the good-bad tradition to heeding my call and trying to fulfill the gifts and talents God had given me to positively impact the world.

Coach Casem often told me, "I had a lot of characters come through here, but none of them was like you, Young. You were my pit bull. I've never seen anyone come in here as mixed up and confused as you were and then end up on the other side of solid. I'm so proud of you." To hear Coach Casem, all those years later, say those things about me meant the world to me. I revered him for years. He was the most well-read, most evolved individual I have ever known. Sadly, we lost Coach Casem in 2020.

The Wake-Up Call

At the beginning of my wake-up call, I wrestled with my newfound consciousness. A new conversation began in my mind, informing me that life should be more intentional than living for the weekend or pursuing the next distraction. Now, I understand that I am living on borrowed time; we all are. I am not here forever. I do not know what day will be my last on earth. Every morning is a chance for gratitude and a chance to build on what I didn't get right the day before. Therefore, I take nothing for granted. I do not live unto myself, but in service to others.

Waking up is the process of realizing your reason for being, the journey to understand that life should be more intentional than looking for a good time or getting up and working a nine-to-five. Human beings were not created to merely labor. Yes, labor is admirable, but within that labor you find your purpose, and that is what ignites your gifts. Through those gifts, others are blessed. Your life, every life, has a specific purpose lived out through the Creator. When you realize that, you accept that your lows are not low lows, they are high lows, and your struggles are not intended to weaken you; they are a gift meant to strengthen you.

The beauty of waking up is that it happens internally. There might be external influences to get you started on your wake-up journey, but the real work happens on the inside. That transformation does not happen by osmosis. Intentional actions of meditation, prayer, and introspective thinking are important parts of the process. This is where you and your Creator commune and live. You must be sober and mature to endure this journey. That is the hardest part, but that is where the breakthrough happens. You have to go inside and ask the hard questions of life. The answers are simple, in that they are hiding in plain sight. At the same time, the process is difficult, in that it requires effort and action by the one driving the car: you.

Essentially, you stumble over simplicity. It is right in front of you, but each day, you overlook it because there is so much noise in the world. This is why quiet time is essential to waking up. During meditation, you tune into your consciousness and experience the therapeutic benefits of self-care. In that space, there's no finger-pointing or blaming. Instead, you question yourself. Who am I, really? Why am I not being all I should be? You reflect on your purpose and allow the Creator to shape your perspective into what it should be.

There is no guarantee that you will magically wake up once you reach a certain age. Instead, there are some life experiences that lead you to it. You begin by living in darkness, going from one mistake to the next with no direction and no focus. Nothing matters to you except getting to the next feel-good thing, and even that does not last long. When you have nothing to anchor you, you don't even realize you need to wake up. You might find yourself in a place you never thought you would be, doing something you're ashamed of with people you thought were your friends, or maybe with people you don't even know. That is when you realize something is wrong, something is missing. You do not recognize this version of yourself and you don't like what you see. You realize you are better than this and you know it's time for a change. You have reached the end of yourself. Now what?

It's time to take massive action. It is time to explore the gifts God has given you. Being intentional about waking up helps you avoid the myriad of things designed to distract you. The best way to avoid those distractions is to develop a routine that includes: 1) daily quiet time, when you just sit in silence; 2) reading and digesting positive information that builds you up, mentally and emotionally; 3) seeking to understand yourself as a spiritual being; and 4) eliminating negative distractions—people, activities, information, and behaviors.

Waking up is as critical as breathing air. We all have a finite time here on this earth, and this is a proving ground. We all come with a purpose, and many things we experience in this life work to distract us from it. That is the struggle. Do not invert the equation and spend your whole life in search of pleasure. Instead, seek first your purpose. Finding it makes you stronger. Develop the courage to know you are worthy to give yourself the best version of who you are created to be. Life is not about the constant search for and indulgence in the things you want. At the same time, when you get a chance to experience the good things, do that and enjoy them to the max. When you laugh, you need to laugh hard. If you find someone to love, love them to the nth degree. When you accept that you have a finite time to live—and in the end, the goal is to figure out why you exist—you become anxious to know who you are and what your gifts are. To do that, you need to wake up.

The moment you wake up, God will alter your way of being. Don't believe me? That's fine. Keep doing life your way. You will learn the truth at the end of your journey because this journey does end for us all. What you withhold from life, life will withhold from you. What you give to life, life gives back to you more than you could ever expect at your time of need. It is your right and your responsibility to wake up.

Clean Up

Luke 15:20 "And he got up and came to his father. But while he was still a long way off, his father saw him and felt compassion for him, and he ran and embraced him, and kissed him. 15:21 And the son said to him, 'Father, I have sinned against heaven and in your sight; I am no longer worthy to be called your son.' 15:22 But the father said to his slaves, 'Quickly bring out the best robe and put it on him, and put a ring on his hand and sandals on his feet;'"

Everyone has baggage. That baggage follows you throughout your life until you unpack it, whether it is a difficult childhood riddled with abuse and abandonment or a mind filled with disappointment over wrong choices, missed opportunities, or low self-esteem. Knowing what to cling to for dear life and what to cast out because it has weighed you down for far too long is a delicate balance. The secret to knowing the difference is revealed as you wake up and your awareness is aroused. At that point, you begin your journey to clean up. Deciding to eliminate things that prevent you from reaching the fullness of who you are is the start of the clean-up process, and it can only happen after you wake up. Eliminating that baggage and making a decision to do and be something different is what cleaning up is all about.

The prodigal son found himself eating with pigs, and after a while, it became normal to him. Then, in the midst of his pain, he heard the voice of the Creator shouting to him. He woke up and decided to clean up, to cast out certain things from his life. The experience that leads to that decision is different for everyone. When my decision point presented itself, I wrestled against it because it interrupted my life. A seed had been planted when I was eleven years old, through my dad, my coaches, and other positive male figures. They represented the Creator whispering to me, but I didn't hear Him then. I could have chosen the good side back then, but I got distracted by the shiny objects that offered me pleasure.

That night with Kemp and his buddies, I was exposed to all the truths I had been running from and the memories I was hiding inside myself. Like the prodigal son, in a moment of realization, I decided to release it all. Thankfully, someone who understood what I was going through offered a way to a clean slate. In my moment of truth, I was convinced that all my screw-ups could be erased and I could get a second chance. The Creator shouted to me through my pain to clean up, as he did to the prodigal son. Eventually, I realized I couldn't take the next step while carrying the baggage. Soon enough, the reality hit me that the clean-up is not one and done; it is a continual process.

Once you clean up, you're ready to go back home—not a physical home, but to your true self, your right mind, and your connection to the Creator, which you severed when the shiny objects of the world caught your attention. Like the prodigal son, you don't know what awaits you when you get home. You might have some shame, some guilt, or something you need to forgive yourself for. Little do you know that your spiritual home is always home and the one who made you is always there waiting for you to come back. It is not the Creator's responsibility to go get you. It's your responsibility to come back to yourself because cleaning up is an inside job. If waking up is about realizing you exist and understanding who and whose you are—and with that, coming to believe in something bigger than yourself—cleaning up has to do with redemption, making amends, deciding to get on the right path to be, do, and live what you know is right.

You begin by looking inside and addressing long overdue weights that hold you down—habits, relationships, behaviors, addictions, shame, guilt, and thoughts. It is a spiritual spring cleaning in a sense. You have to go inside and have hard conversations with yourself about yourself, and you do this without condemning or punishing yourself. In some cases, it requires professional help to unpack some of the baggage. Other times, you can do this on your own. The whole idea is to unpack the baggage and clear out the clutter to discover who you really are.

You clear the clutter by asking yourself some hard questions:
- Who am I?
- What was I designed to do?
- Why am I still here after all the mess I've been through?
- Why am I not the embodiment of what I aspire to be?

- What do I need to remove from my life to be my best self?
- Who have I hurt in my life thus far?
- Who do I want to positively impact going forward?
- Who do I want to be?
- What's next for me in life?

Removing the clutter causes you to think honestly about yourself. It also helps you think more clearly about your future. Once you've done that, you can consider the actions you have to take to move forward in life in a way that's more beneficial to you and to others. Thinking is the most essential part of cleaning up. It is the preparation you need for the next phase—Stand Up—but don't get ahead of yourself. You won't just stand up as your better self and start making things happen. Clean up is a process of checking in, balancing, cleaning, and cleansing. It's hard because it involves patience. You are not going to sweep out everything at one time. This isn't some magic trick where you snap your fingers, say, "Abracadabra!" and then everything is perfect. It doesn't work that way. Some of the stuff you sweep out is going to return.

When I began running marathons later in life, I didn't know what I was doing. I did everything wrong. I would train and run, all with the goal of working my way up to run twenty-two, then twenty-six miles. As I got stronger and built up my endurance, I learned about the mythical twenty-mile wall. That's when you want to quit, when your mind tells you all your training and sacrificing aren't worth the fatigue you're feeling. Your body starts to resist, your legs feel like rubber bands, your brain is in a fog, you start to notice all these distractions, and you want to stop running. That isn't the time to quit. That is the time to push forward.

Cleaning up is like marathon training. You have to keep putting one foot in front of the other and believe everything you've done up to that point has prepared you to cross the finish line. You have to face the flaws you uncover in your character, knowing that doing so leads to the big payoff you are seeking. You have to have a conversation with yourself, to wrestle yourself to the ground, and convince yourself that you are worthy of knowing your true self and of living the life you know you deserve. Just like the marathons, the clean-up process is designed to make you better and better and better. It never stops because there is always more inside you to discover.

The victory is in the overcoming. Leading to the clean-up, you have been tested, you have been put through the fire, and now you are ready to be fortified. You feel good about what you've been through so far simply because you've made it to this point, but the clean-up takes you beyond the good feeling. Now is the time to grow, and growth requires struggle. Each night, when I returned to that dope house, I went inside and wrestled with myself. The struggle was not about me trying to convert the drug guys in that house to know God. It was about me coming to myself. I had to make a declaration in my heart and in my mind. I had to release all the "just in case" possibilities, stop trying to hedge my bets, and go all in. I had to embrace my new self, to decide and declare that I would step into my purpose, not because I was afraid to remain where I was, but because I deserved better. I had come to know that I was created for something else and I had been living beneath my privilege. Once

I declared that, I was able to burn off all the excess; however, there is a struggle that comes with the clean-up.

We are in an imperfect world and in imperfect bodies. As such, we constantly struggle to overcome and understand, essentially to clean up. Minister and evangelist Myles Munroe said the great tragedy of life is that too many of us never acquire insight into our real existence because we shy away from struggle. We think we are entitled to things we're not really entitled to. In fact, we have to wrestle with a thing in order to win it. We make covenants with the things we have chosen to identify with, and we cling to those things throughout our lives until they become part of our belief system, the baggage. On the other hand, we oppose certain things we encounter, and we cast them aside. We build a wall, shut down our minds, and repel those things. When that happens, we cripple ourselves from learning the truth, from growing, and from discovering our purpose.

The life you seek can never be yours until you truly understand the original intent of it. Until you understand that intent, you will live life as less than who you were created to be, and you will always fall short of your best. In a speech delivered in 1857, Frederick Douglass stated, "If there is no struggle, there is no progress." As long as you are here, whether you like it or not, you will struggle. But struggle brings about endurance, which brings about strength, which fortifies you for what's to come. Cleaning up is the preparation for what's next. You cannot skip this part and ever expect to live in the fullness of your purpose.

*Romans **5:3** Not only so, but we also glory in our sufferings, because we know that suffering produces perseverance; **4** perseverance, character; and character, hope. **5** And hope does not put us to shame, because God's love has been poured out into our hearts through the Holy Spirit, who has been given to us."*

Not until the end of my sophomore year did my spiritual awakening expose a new perspective on life and how, when I submitted to the gifts God had given me, I could accomplish just about anything, even when it came with physical or emotional pain. Football, in addition to being a fun outlet for my high energy and an opportunity for a future career, had taught me structured discipline and how to push forward through a problem, even when my body was failing me. After my spiritual awakening, everything became clear in my mind. All I had to do was apply the same principles in the classroom that I was learning in my spiritual walk, and I would get the results I desired. When I activated the discipline and order I learned through understanding the gifts the Creator had given me, and applied them to my studies, I discovered my unique way of learning, which elevated me from academic probation to making the dean's list. I saw this result not because I was brilliant but because of what I had learned from football and through my spiritual awakening. With that, other opportunities opened up for me, some of which changed my life in ways I could have only dreamed of.

A Match Made in Heaven

When I met Kathleen in my freshman year, I was a confused, drug-dealing roughneck. I did not have my act together. I was pretending to be cool, important, a "Li'l Daddy," in other words, an "Uptown Ruler." That first meeting at the library, I was so busy trying to run my usual game on her—the one I'd run on so many other girls—that I didn't notice she was different. She was the first young lady who caught my interest and was truly a young lady. Truth be told, I was intimidated by that. There was nothing to shield her sophisticated eyes from seeing who I really was. I couldn't even pretend to be worthy of the attention and affections of someone as beautiful and intelligent as Kathleen, so I kept my distance from her after that first encounter. I had messed up big because I didn't approach her in a way that was worthy of someone of her caliber. I did not get to know her, learn about her background, or try to uncover her aspirations and interests. All I knew was that she was gorgeous and I wanted to be with her.

We hung out for about a month or so, and then she moved on. Just like that. She wasted no time reaching the conclusion that I was not the kind of guy with whom she wanted to invest her time. She set me straight in a hurry and caused me to show up differently, almost with a reverence, when I reintroduced myself to her years later. For some girls, initially, bad boys are attractive; however, girls who have something going for themselves know how to see through the B.S. That stuff gets old in a hurry. Kathleen was going places, and back then, I wasn't in the right position to go with her.

By the time I reached my junior year, I was a different person. I had cleaned up my act, and I was on sound footing. I had raised my academic standing and created a solid place for myself on the football field. At that time, I was the talk of the campus because I had gone from an outright thug to a religious nut. I was like those guys who go to prison and get that jailhouse religion. I walked around campus with my books in one hand and my Bible in the other. Anyone who came up to me for a conversation had to endure the same thing: "Hey, how ya been? You need Christ as your savior." I would rip that religious tract out, open my Bible, and start debating with them.

Looking back, it must have been quite hilarious. Really, I should have been ashamed of myself for that approach, but it was part of my clean-up journey. My fan club, composed of the Christian girls I met in Bible study, seemed to admire my method of reeling in new meat. To some of them, I was a superstar, a nice and decent guy. They accepted that I had transformed from an outcast into someone who had lost his mind to religion. On the other hand, the girls I'd previously hung out with at parties, all thought my religious act was phony. They would snicker and ask, "Hey, Roynell, how's God doing today?" Then, they would chuckle as I walked past. It didn't bother me because I was in a different place. I was charged up on this newfound thing. Their goal was to break me, to get me in a situation where they could show me up and prove this new me wasn't the real deal. I never let that happen. Once again, my all-in personality showed out, only this time it kept me *from* the drama rather than leading me *to* it. I still had my eyes on Kathleen, and so did every other guy on campus.

Kathleen and I were in physical science class together and I'd sit behind her. I was still intimidated by her and unsure how to approach her the right way because that scene from the library a few years earlier still haunted me. One day, the professor called out a question to the class and announced he would give extra credit to the student who could answer it correctly. Hoping to impress Kathleen, I called out an answer. She proceeded to correct me, right there in front of the entire class. I couldn't have that, so we started bickering.

We carried on for a few minutes before the professor finally said, "Cut it out, Roynell and Kathleen. You don't need to disrupt my class and put on this big act. Everybody knows you two are sweet on each other." I could have dug a hole and crawled into it. "That's not the way you get her," he continued. "You need to just ask her out for dinner." The beauty of attending an HBCU is that everybody is like family. People get all up in your business and keeping a secret is hard. If the mothers in the neighborhood where I grew up spread the news like CNN, the crowd at an HBCU was like Twitter. Of course, the entire class had a good laugh, and I heard about that for a couple weeks every time I passed classmates in the hall.

I finally got up the nerve to ask her out. That was one of the hardest things I did that year. She was beautiful, intelligent, self-assured, and no-nonsense. I was scared, but hopeful she would accept. She played her cards close to her vest. She made me work hard to win her affections, and I don't blame her. Kathleen was on schedule to graduate soon and then move on to a professional career. She did not want a thug-turned-religious-nut, who had a whole year of studies to complete, hanging on her arm. Thankfully, she said yes, and we agreed on a date, but not a place.

In the days leading up to our date, Alcorn played South Carolina State. I had a great game and we won. After the game, the coach came up to me and shook my hand and said he had never seen that kind of defensive back play. That let me know I stood out, and it felt good, not only for that one game, but also because a pro scout from the Los Angeles Rams had come to Alcorn to scout me. He had attended an HBCU too, and somehow he had heard whispers about Kathleen and me. As I said, at an HBCU, everyone is family.

"Look, man," he said, "I know how it is being at a school like this, so I know what you're going through." I had no idea what he was talking about. "We're not supposed to do this, so don't tell anybody. I'm only doing this because I'm sure you're going to end up in the NFL." My curious gaze turned to surprise when he handed me $25 cash. It was to take Kathleen to dinner. Scouts were not allowed to give athletes money to try to influence or recruit them, so doing that could have put us both in jeopardy. Back then, however, that kind of money could buy a nice dinner at a nice restaurant. I was speechless. This would be the first time I had been on a real date. My high school prom was only practice. This time the training wheels were off.

With little experience in how to treat a classy girl, and a gut full of nervous energy, I decided to take her to Steak and Ale in nearby Vicksburg. Not the fanciest place, but it was ideal for us to sit down, eat a good meal, and talk, and I was glad to be able to pay for it. When I picked her up, I was ready to turn on the charm. I had Al Jarreau's "Look to the Rainbow" playing in my car, and I was ready to be a real gentleman, but that all changed as soon as we walked into the restaurant. To my surprise, the hostess area was full of the players and coaches from South Carolina State, the team we had just beaten. They were all right there at the doorway waiting to be seated.

I had this drop-down, pretty girl on my arm and was suddenly faced with this. My mind raced with a scenario in which the night ended in a violent scuffle, my face and knuckles bloodied, and Kathleen watching in horror, after which she would vow to never speak to me again. Even though I was displaying this new me, I was still a product of my upbringing and my environment. My past dictated that was how these kinds of things ended. Silently, I was bracing for another Gregory McGee experience, with me being Greg this time. The conditioning process that was stuffed down inside me from years of living in chaos threatened to make me a product of that history. What I imagined looked less like a welcoming scene from the movie *Black Panther* and more like the tragedy of *Boyz n the Hood*. I quickly shook off that image and decided to leave. Being with Kathleen was more important to me than standing up to a bunch of jocks.

Just as I was about to turn around and walk out, the coach recognized me and waved me over to him at the front of the crowd. I hesitated for a second, then walked forward. The players parted like the Red Sea and let Kathleen and me walk to the front. "Come on up here with your lady," the coach said. As I passed through the sea of players, I felt several pats on the back and heard them say, "Great game, man." My body braced for a last-minute gut punch, but it never came. I exhaled. It was like the prodigal son coming home, the pride waiting for me.

Then, a voice in my mind said, "This is why you went through all that you went through." What a relief. There is nothing like being affirmed by people who are truly on your side. They were genuinely welcoming. They showed me the ultimate respect and that felt great. It was a really sweet moment. Kathleen had a big, beautiful smile on her face. She was so poised and graceful, and I was proud to be with her. We enjoyed our meal, had a nice conversation, and then left. I dropped her off at her place, then cranked up my JBL system, playing Harold Melvin's "If You Don't Know Me by Now" as I drove back to my dorm. I was on cloud nine.

That night, I felt what so many young men are seeking today—power. Too often, what they end up with is toxic power, a violent power, where someone has to lose and where each side tries to make sure it's not them. What they do not understand is that they can get the respect and the power they're seeking when they do the right thing. That is the arrival point of the clean-up. The baggage of the past has been left behind, you hold your chin up because you have faced your demons, and you walk erect because you know you are not perfect but you're a proud work in progress. That is when people respect you and want to honor you. That feels good.

From that point on, Kat and I were like two peas in a pod, inseparable. This was my reward for cleaning up my act. The rest, as they say, is history.

Clean-up is all about developing your character and seeking balance. If you don't consistently clean up, you run the risk of being defined by your past and the environment you live in, rather than defining yourself based on what the Creator is showing you through the experiences of your life. As you look behind at the baggage you've let go of through clean-up, you begin to transcend your current circumstances and envision yourself anew. You start to analyze what you need to go forward as opposed to constantly reacting to the messages coming at you. Those messages come from everywhere, constantly.

Every reasonable human adult knows they need to clean up. Sadly, most wait until New Year's Eve to begin the clean-up process. In some ways, New Year's resolutions are a utopian crutch. You have to find your reason for being and then declare it, not because of some magical date or time of year, but because you are connected to your reason for being. Declaration drives effort, which all goes back to finding a deep reason for being. Waiting until life hits you so hard that you are forced to clean up makes the job that much harder.

Decide to clean up, not because someone else thinks it's a good idea or because you're trapped in a living hell, but because you know life has more for you than what you are currently experiencing. If you decide to wait until you get to the end of your rope before you clean up—and many people do—that's okay too, but you don't have to wait. Civil Rights icon Fannie Lou Hamer said, "I'm sick and tired of being sick and tired." You don't have to get to that point in order to clean up your life. Have the courage to do it every single day. The clean-up starts with a hunger for something better, even if you do not know what that is or how to get there.

When you ask yourself if you have to wait to die to experience heaven, or if you can have some of it while you're living, your conscience speaks to you that you can have it now. You might not believe what your conscience says, and you might decide to drown it out with distractions, like people, activities, music, drugs, whatever. What you should do instead is lean into it and allow it to amplify. When that happens, you equip yourself to find the courage to clean up so you can live out your purpose. This is not an easy task. You risk being ostracized and ridiculed. In most cases, you're not celebrated for it, at least not in the beginning, but that's okay. Accept the reality that you will never reach perfection and decide simply to live out God's purpose in your life. Surrender to it, but keep your balance because there will always be a gravitational pull to the other side.

The clean-up helps you clear the clutter in your life so you can see what needs to be done. You start building. You fortify yourself. And you keep doing it because cleaning up is a perpetual process. Life goes on and you face the same ups and downs you did before, but now you have a different perspective. You're out of the darkness and can see more clearly. You know who you are. You've come to terms with your past because you've left the baggage at the door. You are ready to walk into a new version of yourself, unencumbered by any shame or guilt. Just like with the wake-up, when you clean up, you understand your lows are not low lows, they're high lows. So even when you dip, you're not in a valley. You realize you are more than a survivor; you're a warrior. That is the invitation to stand up.

Stand Up

*Luke 15:23 "'And bring the fattened calf
and kill it, let us eat and be merry. 15:24 for
this son of mine was dead and has come to
life again; he was lost, and has been found.'
And they began to be merry."*

Once you wake up and clean up, it's time to stand up. Standing up is a matter of equipping yourself to break away from the gravitational pull and the opinions of others. When you reach this point, no one can shame you into being less than who you are and what you were created to be. Standing up is unapologetically walking in your purpose and focusing on something bigger than yourself. When you know there is something bigger to hope for, your life gains volume and substance. Standing up takes you beyond yourself. Your new persona creates a vapor that envelops others, and oftentimes they don't even recognize the impact. It frees other people, ignites them, influences them, and allows them to define purpose in their own living.

When I first read the parable of the prodigal son, I was mad that this story had been hidden from me. Without question, I knew it was the definitive story of my life, the perfect depiction of a guy like me who had everything to live for, had left it all behind out of selfish motives, found himself in the pig pen of life, and then woke up, cleaned up, humbled himself, and returned home, where he could stand up and be who his Creator had called him to be. It beautifully illustrated my journey from darkness, and promised an abundance of hope on the other side. In darkness, I viewed life as a binary activity. It was a zero-sum game. I would either lose or I'd win. I did not understand that part of winning is falling down and being graced with the ability to get back up. I figured once the bottom falls out, that's the end of the game.

Learning the truth, that I wouldn't always get things right, helped me see that my life is not lived in bubble wrap. I am not protected from failure. In fact, failure is sometimes a necessary and essential part of this life, so the shame in failure dissipated. Living a purpose-filled life allowed me to not beat up on myself, to take ownership of my thoughts and actions, to be gentle with myself, and to forgive my own mistakes and missteps. I learned to use the downs as an exercise to prepare for the next thing I'd have to step into that would be larger than anything I had experienced. I no longer panicked. I learned to just be. That only happened once I decided to stand up and be the best version of myself.

Mothers know things; they just do. It's intuition, I guess. When my mother realized I had met someone, she was real smooth about it. "Who's the lucky girl?" she asked during one of my visits home from college. She was standing in the living room, watching me unpack my suitcase. I had planned to be home for a few days, so I wanted to set my things out. I had never talked about Kat to my family, never sent home pictures, never even acted all lovey-dovey in front of them, from what I could tell. As far as I was concerned, I was the same guy who had left home, minus my knucklehead behavior.

"What are you talking about, Mom?" Sometimes, you can get people to believe whatever they're thinking is all wrong. You can fool some of the people some of the time, but you can't fool ya mama none of the time.

"Oh, I can tell you're dating somebody," she said, tilting her head to the side and turning up the corners of her mouth. "All your clothes are folded and neat, and they smell fresh. I know you didn't do that. That's a woman's touch." She laughed, and I couldn't help but blush. I was busted.

The spring before my senior year, Kat was set to graduate summa cum laude from Alcorn, but I had another year before I finished my studies. The NFL draft was right around the corner, and I was poised as a top pick, so I was willing to leave Alcorn a year early if a pro team offered me a fair shot. She was preparing to go to Chicago after graduating to start a career as a case worker for a large hospital, and I was in full support. We agreed that we would grow independent of each other for a year or two after college and then reconnect to begin our life together. Emotionally and spiritually, we were committed to each other, and we were all but engaged, but we hadn't formalized anything. We both wanted to make sure our next step together in life was mature and informed rather than impulsive. The fact that we both had a lot of opportunity in front of us made the decision easy.

That January, I'd gone on interviews with different teams—Dallas, New York, Chicago, Atlanta, Tampa Bay—so they could inspect me and I could meet the coaching staff. They were feeling me out to see if I was a good fit. Around that time, the New Orleans Saints invited me for an interview. My mind went back to when I thought I would attend Tulane. I felt like my hometown was embracing me, and that felt great.

I invited Kat to drive down with me so she could meet my family. I knew they would take her in and treat her like one of their own. The entire drive from Mississippi to New Orleans was nice. Kat and I talked and laughed. She asked me all kinds of questions about my parents, my siblings, my neighborhood. I don't know which one of us was more excited about her meeting my family. When we arrived at my mom's house, I looked over at Kat before we got out of the car and asked, "Are you ready?" She smiled, and I knew she had no idea what she was in for.

When we walked inside the small shotgun house, the entire place lit up and suddenly turned into a celebration. Everyone was there—my mother, my grandmother, people from the neighborhood—talking loud and hugging us. "Oh, she's a pretty girl!" my mom said loud enough for everyone in the house to hear. My grandmother got up and hugged Kat real tight, and I was swept away by my brothers to hang out on the front porch. Meanwhile, I noticed my three sisters in the corner glancing over and whispering. I figured they were sizing up Kat and deciding which one of them would be the first to approach her on their recognizance mission to learn more about this girl I had brought home. My sisters—Michelle, Pie, and Val—were overly critical and overprotective of me, but I knew they would love Kat, and I was eager to see how they would embrace her. Kat has a warmth and an earthiness that can charm and disarm just about anyone, so I knew she could handle herself with them.

As things settled down, my sisters made their way over to Kat, who was sitting quietly on the couch. I peeked into the house to see if she was okay, glanced away for a few minutes, and then looked back in her direction to see them all laughing like lifelong friends. They were telling stories about me. Pie, the alpha female, led the conversation. Michelle, the loving soul she is, embraced Kat in a sisterly way. Val, in her shy way, soaked it all up to use the information later. They had no idea Kat had performed a Jedi mind trick on them and they were caught in her trap. She's always had that way about herself. My dad came by the house later and immediately fell in love with Kat. "She's got that blow-in-the-wind kind of hair," was all he said to me. That was enough to let me know he approved.

Kathleen's first visit to New Orleans to meet my family

The Saints invited me for brunch at the famous Court of Two Sisters restaurant in the French Quarter so we could talk about the possibility of me joining the team. All the excitement around the Saints considering me for the NFL draft caused the local folks to lose their minds. I had been named the Black College Defensive Player of the Year and an All-American Player of the Year. The rumor mill and sports talk shows were hungry for a good story, and their eagerness for me to be the focal point began to ruin my cover. It was too much for me. I just wanted to bring my girl home to meet the family, train with the Saints for a few days, and keep my head down until I either finished college or was drafted.

People at home thought I had already made it to the big league when, in fact, all I had to my name was $20 and a ten-speed bike that I rolled around town on because I didn't have gas money for my car. That's how I showed up to Shakespeare Park for my training routine, the same workout I did to get ready for Alcorn. Sadly, the same winos were hanging out in the bleachers, just like they had been years ago when I was in high school. All the interviews and training were in preparation for the big day—NFL Draft Day—and it was right around the corner.

I went back to campus, and there was a huge energy surge around the possibility of me being not just a draft choice, but a first-round draft choice, something that lends itself to bragging rights. The teams I'd visited with had made a lot of promises, but nothing was guaranteed. I was dazed and confused. I had to protect myself both from the hype and from being disappointed. I could not risk the emotional investment of believing any of it, so I shut out all the noise and continued with life as usual, as if none of the excitement existed.

I had already experienced loss, disappointment, and dejection in my life, and I wouldn't allow myself the indulgence of believing I could actually become an NFL player. The last thing I wanted was to nurse and rehearse the outcome, get my hopes up, and then be disappointed, so I refused to engage in the fantasy of living my dream. Not that dreams are bad, but I knew I had to dream soberly. I had done everything I could do to ensure the dream happened, but the decision was out of my hands, so I redirected that energy to something I could control.

That experience taught me the importance of having multiple options, several irons in the fire, in a sense. Focusing on one thing is fine, sometimes. Other times, being able to explore and exploit multiple talents is more advantageous because it moves me outside my comfort zone. My attention turned to my studies because I could control that and influence the outcome based on my input.

As draft day drew near, the tension was palpable. By then, I had an agent, and he secretly flew me to Houston, where I stayed at his house to hide out and escape the fanfare. We went to dinner the night before the draft, after which I said my prayers and went to bed. The next morning, the draft started bright and early, but I didn't know what was going on because cable TV and the news media weren't what they are today. We were not able to follow the developments moment by moment, so we listened to the draft on sports radio all day and stayed close to a phone to await a call that I hoped would be good news.

I was engaged, but not overly so. My mind was in a fog and I was emotionally cautious, still reluctant to believe the outcome I wanted could actually happen. Throughout the day, I got a few phone calls from different teams, dangling carrots in front of me. "Okay, Young, get ready. We've got the next pick and we're going to draft you." Then, I would hear on the radio that that team had made their selection and it wasn't me. I didn't know who or what to believe at that point. Finally, I decided to check out.

After a few teams had taken their pick in the first round, my agent said, "Hey, Philadelphia is on the board. They have the twenty-third pick. Let's see what they'll do." Until that point, Philadelphia had not shown their hand to me like the other teams had. I'd visited with the Eagles, just like I had done with the others, but they were quiet and seemed uninterested in me. I later realized that was part of their plan. Jackie Graves, a legendary, old-school scout for the Eagles, knew all about how things worked at HBCUs. He knew where the talent was, and he influenced the Eagles to consider me. But he was stealth and went out of his way to hide me from the limelight. Even in the all-star games, he influenced the coaches to play me in a position that wasn't my normal position, which I thought was strange at the time. As it turned out, that was part of his plan.

As each team announced their first-round pick and my name wasn't called, I decided that, as long as I got drafted, I was good. Meanwhile, the agent kept telling me the money is better in the first round, so that added more pressure to my mind and more knots in my stomach. About thirty minutes passed, and my phone rang. It was the general manager from the Philadelphia Eagles.

"Roynell, I want to welcome you to the Eagles and let you know that you've been our first-round draft choice selection. Here's coach Dick Vermeil." I wasn't sure if I should believe him. It had been an emotionally tumultuous morning, and I desperately wanted to believe this was the victorious finale of a drama in which I was the leading character. As it turned out, it was. Coach Vermeil and I talked briefly, and as soon as we hung up, things exploded. The next call was a media rep, who said he had a pool of journalists ready to ask me questions. It would be an understatement to say I was unprepared. My brain went from zero to one hundred in a matter of seconds, and I had to rely on my wit to get through it all. "How does it feel? Are you surprised you were picked in the first round? Were the Eagles your first choice? What does your family have to say?" The questions were being fired at me like bullets from a machine gun. It was overwhelming, but I held my own. The dream had become a reality.

Two days later, I flew with my agent to Philadelphia, ready to meet the coaching staff and get my bearings in this organization that had selected me. There I was, a kid from New Orleans, who had just been drafted into the NFL. It felt good, but I still felt like myself, not like some kind of celebrity.

We landed in Philadelphia, and as the plane taxied to the gate, the flight attendant began making the final announcements. "Welcome to Philadelphia International Airport. Please gather all of your belongings as you prepare to exit the aircraft. Upon arrival at the gate, please remain seated because we have a special passenger who needs to disembark. The Philadelphia Eagles first-round draft choice, Roynell Young!" Everyone on the plane applauded and cheered. I sunk down into my seat, completely embarrassed. Sheepishly, I got up to deplane. From that point forward, I no longer had privacy. People would follow me and ask for my autograph. I couldn't have a private conversation anymore. That part of becoming a professional athlete was the least appealing of all.

The meeting with the Eagles went well. I met the coaches and a few players and got some insight into their game plan going forward. As it turned out, the Eagles had been in the playoffs the prior year. They got close to being the NFC East champions, but they were missing a key player. I learned that I was that missing piece. The Eagles had never drafted a cornerback in the first round, so their investment in me was huge. Equally important, Alcorn had never had anyone drafted in the first round. That was an honor, but it was a lot of weight to carry. I wanted to represent my hometown and shed a positive light on my university, especially since it was an HBCU. However, I did not want to go into professional sports and come out all chopped up, broke, and broken down like I had seen happen to other players. I rebelled against all the hype and went deep inside myself to work out how I would be in this new space.

I had enough sense to know you only celebrate once you succeed, and I had not succeeded yet. I was just getting started and still had a lot to prove to the Eagles and to myself. So I tapped into the wisdom of the ancestors to protect me. I was very cautious with my image and with my money. I wasn't flashy. I knew better because, as far as I was concerned, I was the underdog. I hadn't come up where people preferred me, where I was nurtured to be my best and play better than everyone else. I remembered my middle school coach telling me, "We don't have a suit to fit you, Young." I was never part of the in crowd, never voted most likely to succeed. I was always the guy who crashed the party and had to fight my way in.

Like my first year in college, no one was grooming me for what was ahead. This time, that worked in my favor because it played into my personality. I did not want to be famous or popular. I'm a loner by nature. I wanted to make the money and compete on the field, but I wasn't pursuing the other things that come with a big paycheck. Most people didn't understand my persona. They thought I should be enjoying all the benefits this newfound fame would bring me. All I knew was that now I had to watch my back because I didn't know who to trust.

Back home in New Orleans with Kat for a few months, I was hanging out at the house, working out, and minding my own business, when out of the blue, the Philadelphia Eagles called me to come out to their mini-training camp. I thought I would have a few more months before training started, but I was excited to get an early feel for what things would be like with the team. With Kat and my family getting along well, and her preparing to go off to Chicago to start her career, I felt comfortable leaving her there to go out to Philly for a few days.

Mini-camp is a three-day, super-intense workout where the team essentially kicks the tires to see what they've bought. The first three years of my contract were guaranteed, so I felt pretty good, but I still wanted to show up strong. They put all the new players in an artificial bubble, where we had an intense download of complex plays, went through daily mock scrimmages, and essentially performed so the coaching staff could see how well each person would adapt to the complexities of the NFL.

The guy I roomed with didn't get drafted; he was a free agent. The first night after practice, I went to the room to study the plays, but he wasn't there. He was out clubbing. The second night, they slid a pink slip under the door for him, and they came in the next morning to pack his stuff and send him on his way. He did it to himself. No amount of talent can position you if you do not stand up and do your part. You have to earn your place in the world. Watching him leave, I thought, *Some guys can't get out of their own way*. He wasn't the only one. Over those few days, I learned some guys came prepared and some guys came entitled. That was my moment to stand up in the place I had dreamed of and worked hard for. Given my missteps as a youth, I was thankful to no longer be wrestling with that old baggage.

Training camp was hard, but I could handle the physical part. I didn't know it yet, but I had trained for it most of my life—from that day smacking that kid's face into the pavement at Thomy Lafon School to tough tackles at Alcorn. What I had not trained for were the additional distractions that come with life as a professional athlete, what some would call the fruits of my labor. At that point, I was trying to establish myself, so I developed tunnel vision. I wanted to be on the straight and narrow in every way, and I knew a setup when I saw one.

One night, after a long day of training, I got back to the hotel and the lobby was full of women with suitcases and fancy clothes. I thought they were checking in to attend a women's conference or something. They looked nice, but I had no energy to be interested. One young lady came up close to me, and suddenly, I was surrounded by four or five others. I started pushing my way through like they were flies because I knew what was going on. I thought to myself, *It's going to be a long year, in more ways than one.* I have always had a pretty healthy opinion of myself, and my low-key arrogance protected me from a lot of unintended situations with women, but this was over the top.

As these ladies continued to swarm around me and my teammates, one said, "That's okay, he can act shy for now, but we'll catch him at the library." My mind quickly flashed to the library at Alcorn, where I had tried to corner Kat into giving me her number all those years ago. That confused me because none of those women looked like the intellectual type. I could look in their eyes and tell all they saw were dollar signs. I glanced over at one of my future teammates, and he explained that The Library was a nightclub and the ladies were expecting me to be there that night. Crazy thing was I did not want any part of that scene. I was feeling good about what I saw with the Eagles, plus things were going well with Kat and me, and I didn't want to blow my chances with her. Besides that, I was partied out at that point, and I was not going to lower myself to that level.

There I was, young, gifted, and Black, and denying myself the pleasures being served up to me. It was flattering but also frustrating. I wanted to tell those ladies they were shaming themselves and their families. Far be it from me to knock someone's hustle, but I was not about to go down like that. I knew if I dipped into the fruits of fame at that point, I would eventually succumb to those pleasures and that would ultimately result in an outcome I would regret—losing Kat or having a child out of wedlock with some woman I barely knew. I was on a mission to stand up as the man I had grown into, determined to make this opportunity with the Philadelphia Eagles a launching pad for whatever was next in my life. I was not about to blow it.

When I got to my room, I was exhausted. I lay on the bed and told myself I would not return to Philly unless I had a companion with me. I couldn't survive that lifestyle alone. Somebody—my mama, my sister, somebody—had to come up there and live with me. I realized then that choosing the right mate is crucial to survival when you stand up. I needed Kathleen to be there for me as someone I could retreat to, someone to keep me sane and sober. She had been my ride or die, and I knew we made a good team. I was ready to make sure she'd always be there for me.

When I returned to New Orleans, Kat seemed to be fitting in quite well with my family. She was hanging out, getting New Orleans-ized. My grandmother had been teaching her all these recipes, and Kat was quickly becoming part of the family. On a beautiful day in May, she and I went for a walk. "Look, Kat, let's ditch the plan," I blurted out, as we strolled through City Park. She looked curious, shocked because we really didn't have a plan. "We don't know what's going to happen in the next two years with you in Chicago and me in Philly. So let's just go ahead and get married."

She smiled and said, "Well, yeah, that's fine. We can start planning and maybe do it over the summer, then—"

Before she could finish, I said, "I've got an idea. You want to get married today?"

"Are you serious?" We had stopped walking and stood there smiling at each other.

"All right!" she said, and then she wrapped her arms around my neck, and we kissed.

We went to straight to City Hall for the blood test. When they told us it would take a few days for the official paperwork to be completed, I was a little disappointed, but we figured that was fine. During those few days, we didn't tell anyone what we were up to, but once the documents were officially filed at City Hall, it was game on. I told my mom, "Kat and I are getting married today." Out of the blue, I just blurted it out.

"What?" she said. "We knew you were going to get married in a year or two, but not this soon. Are you serious? Today?" She was shocked, but excited. She started asking me all these questions about where we were getting married, who was going to be in the wedding, what about the food, the cake, and all that.

I just stood there and laughed. "We're doing it today, Mom, in about an hour."

Kat and I had decided we didn't want all the fluff. Where I come from, people who have the least, put on the biggest show. That has never been my nature, Kat's either. We decided to keep it low key, but when my family realized we were serious, they went into overdrive. They cleaned up that house so fast I couldn't believe it. Kat and I left to take care of some things, and by the time we returned, my sister had fixed up her prom dress for Kat to wear. My Aunt Jackie gave her an old, worn-out wedding band. I got out my one suit, my go-to dress-up suit, which I had bought from Rubenstein's Men's Store years earlier. My Uncle Earl went down to the neighborhood bakery to get the wedding cake. The rest of the food was no problem because in New Orleans people can cook up something faster than you can say "wedding." My dad came over after work as proud as he could be. I asked a friend who was a minister to officiate, and Kemp Johnson was my best man. The ceremony, held in my mom's living room, took all of thirty minutes and cost about $25. It was perfect.

My $25 wedding has lasted 41 years and counting

Joyce, Roynell, Kathleen, and Wallace Young

When we all exited that little shotgun house, the entire neighborhood was outside. They were hot. There were over a hundred people standing in the street mad as hell because they felt cheated out of celebrating with me. They knew me. I had grown up there. They wanted to share that special moment with our family, but that wasn't how I rolled. That wasn't me.

After our wedding in the shotgun living room, Kat and I figured we'd go back to normal and hang out at the house for the next few days. That was a little naive, even for me. In the midst of all the laughter and celebrating, my mom walked over to me and quietly slipped some money into the palm of my hand. I looked at her, puzzled, and then I unfolded the bills to find $30.

"Son, you just got married," she said. "You can't stay here tonight."

My new bride and I ended up staying at some seedy motel for the night. It was so bad we could hear the roaches scrambling across the linoleum floor. It wasn't ideal, and we both knew it would not be the high mark in our marriage, but there we were. That was May 19th, Malcolm X's birthday and the day the riots broke out in Liberty City, Florida. We watched the mayhem unfold on TV that night.

The next day, we couldn't get out of that roach motel fast enough, and we headed to Thibodaux to spend the weekend with my Grandma Gibbs. She treated Kat like she was a million dollars. Uncle Herbert, my dad's brother, and other family members came by, and I introduced Kat to them. We fellowshipped and feasted on filet of redfish with creole seasonings, all the sides, and homemade ice cream. My grandmother made us feel like we were in a five-star hotel. Being around my elders was a place of honor for me, and Kat blended right in. They loved her from the moment they met her. I knew then that I was ready to stand up and be the man I had been preparing to be all my life.

By the time I arrived in Philadelphia to prepare for pre-season training camp, I was clear-eyed and felt truly liberated and autonomous. I had my beautiful wife there with me, a promising career, and my independence. I was ready to take agency over my life. That was due in part to what waking up and cleaning up had afforded me. I was in position to stand up as a man who had been through some trials of life at an early age and had learned lessons that would shape my every decision going forward. I knew I could not rest on my laurels. A lot was expected of me, and the Eagles made it clear early on that this wouldn't be an easy ride. This was not college ball; it was a business called professional football, the NFL, and the Eagles were gunning for 1981 to be the year they would go to the Super Bowl. The pressure was on me to be their secret weapon, and all eyes were looking in my direction to see if I could stand up, step up, and meet the expectations of the team's management.

As the weeks went on, I thought I was doing well on the field, but the general manager didn't feel that way. Coach Vermeil hadn't let on that anything was wrong, so I figured I was keeping up my end of the bargain. I later learned why Coach Vermeil was in my corner, pushing me to be my best. As one in a string of coaches who knew exactly what I needed at any given time in my football career, he saw that I needed a certain kind of motivation to reach my highest potential.

If my high school football coach, Audrich provided nurturing for me, and my college coach, Casem provided the hard-nosed discipline I needed, Coach Vermeil provided a mixture of both. He was demanding and also nurturing of me and every player, maybe because he saw the entire team as a big family. We were all doing something together, so we had to work together. What I learned from him is that character matters. Some guys had more talent and skill, but according to Coach Vermeil what really mattered was when someone did the little things when nobody was watching. He demonstrated that doing the right thing is required all the time, not just sometimes. His personality influenced my leadership style and taught me to find commonality in diverse groupings of people, but I didn't learn that right away.

One day, I was called in to talk with Coach Vermeil and the general manager. I had shown up to practice on time each day, worked my tail off on the field, and studied my plays. Whatever this meeting was about, I was sure it had nothing to do with my performance, but I was wrong. There we were in the GM's office. Coach Vermeil was unusually quiet, and the GM did all the talking. "Look, Young, let me get straight to the point. We have a lot riding on you, and you're not living up to our expectations." I was speechless. "We brought you in with the expectation that you would bring a lot more than what we've seen from you so far. I think you're holding back. This isn't college ball. You'd better get it together out there on the field."

I swallowed hard and dealt with it. He was a straight talker and I appreciated that. I didn't know exactly what more I could do, but I knew I had to figure it out in a hurry. They had goals and I was a big part of that. They did not have time for me to be a rookie. They needed me to be a pro, and quickly. It was a shaky start, and it was the truth I needed to hear. The more I thought about his words, the more I realized he was right. I needed to stand up in the role I had been hired to perform. I was a pro now, and I couldn't get away with the hard-charging, ultra-physical way I'd played in college. I was all about making the defensive hits back then and showing my strength. In pro sports, there's more to it than that. Soon enough, I found a way to alter the way I played, and my game became more cerebral than physical.

I had a strong belief in myself and I was determined to prevail. Coach Sid Gilman, a quarterbacks coach, who even then was an icon in the NFL, said something to me that changed my whole view of things and got me on the right track. I liked him a lot because he had style, swag. He was a clothes horse like I was. He would dress in three-piece tweed suits, like Elliot Ness in *The Untouchables*, topped off with a fedora and carrying an alligator briefcase. He was sharp. During our pre-season game against New England, my game started to click, and I was getting into my groove. Afterward, Coach Gilman walked up to me in the locker room and said, "Young, man, I just want to let you know you belong in this league and you're going to have a long career in the NFL. You're a player. You belong." It felt so good to hear him say that. His words gave me an extra push to keep going.

As the season progressed, we went on to play New Orleans in the Super Bowl. I felt good knowing I was a vital piece to that puzzle and I had played an active part to positively impact my team. Had I not done the work to search my soul and improve my game, I would have doubted myself. I had done the work, so I was able to stand up.

Having Kat there with me as the sole member of my posse meant everything. We were a solid team, and she was my confidant and my support system. My nature is to be a loner, so I wasn't interested in the fan clubs and groupies some of the other guys had surrounding them. My life was just Kat and me, and it was perfect. Soon enough, I learned I would become a father, and I was over the moon. Everything was coming together, and our little tribe was rounding out.

Despite being what most would consider a celebrity athlete, I did not feel that way. I was still me, a regular guy from New

Orleans who had messed up, cleaned up, worked hard, and now found myself living the dream a lot of young athletes have. I didn't leverage all the trimmings that come with that lifestyle, and I was fine with that. I did not allow myself to be exposed to the kinds of activities that would be a distraction for me. Football was just a job, and I was an enigma, even to myself, but it protected me from falling victim to negative things or people who didn't have my best interests at heart.

I did not consider myself lucky. I knew I was blessed. My Creator had allowed me to go through some things that led me to this place of favor, where I could stand up and be something more than I ever thought I could be. I wasn't sure what that was, but I knew it wasn't just for me. Somehow, I knew in my heart that my life's purpose was bigger than the NFL.

While in Philadelphia, I began to experience all the things associated with living in a large, metropolitan city. I lived in a high-rise apartment with a great view downtown on Walnut Street. There were professionals and maybe a few celebrities who lived there too; I never encountered any, but I'm sure they were there. I always had a haunting voice in my head that it could all go away, so I didn't get too comfortable. Because I was a city dweller—unlike the majority of the guys I played with, who lived in the suburbs—I enjoyed riding the subway to and from the stadium. Being on public transportation separated me from the contrived world of professional football—with money and comforts to cushion against real life—and allowed me to be among real people, to decompress. It was my way of staying anchored and humble. Most onlookers—teammates, coaches, or even people I encountered in public—didn't understand that.

There were times when people recognized me on the subway and they were shocked by my presence there.

One day, while riding the subway home from the stadium, a guy sitting next to me recognized me and said, "Hey, you play for the Eagles. What are you doing riding the subway?"

I smiled and looked down. It always amused me to see how people reacted to me taking public transportation. I was never comfortable with the hero worship thing. This guy seemed almost uncomfortable, as if I was taking up space that belonged to someone else. "I'm going home from work," I said. "That's what I'm doing here!"

That interaction exposed me to the reality that, even though I did not see myself as different from other people, they saw me as somehow separate from them. Despite that, I chose to stand in who I was and not conform to what they thought I should be. I was a working man, just like he was, and really, all I did was go to work and go home. That was my life. I avoided all the razzle-dazzle of the limelight of being a pro athlete and just laid low. Funny thing is, laying low was a huge part of me standing up, or *standing in* who I had become. I wouldn't say I was super conscious of it, but I had become what we would call back in the day a stand-up kind of guy. I had a promising career, a beautiful wife, a kid on the way, and a solid relationship with my Creator. I was good with who I was, even if it rubbed some people the wrong way.

A Stand-Up Dad

Standing up requires you to finish what you start, and I had some unfinished business I needed to take care of. After my first season in the NFL, I decided to return to Alcorn to finish my studies and get my degree. Kat had graduated a year earlier, and I was so proud of her. By now, she was seven months pregnant, and I wanted my kid to come into this world with two parents who were college graduates and who valued education. I only needed three classes and twelve hours to finish, so in the summer of 1981, Kat and I moved back to New Orleans to be near my family, and I went off to Alcorn to finish my coursework. I figured if I put my head down and plowed through, I could finish a semester during the summer, which would be perfect timing for me to get back to Philly for the start of training camp.

At first, my return to school was a bit off-putting to some people because they didn't know how to react to me. I moved into the dormitory with the other students, and it was a weird experience for them. There I was, a professional athlete, back in school and seemingly trying to pick up where I had left off. People felt uncomfortable around me, but for me it was humbling. Some professors didn't know how to react to me because they had their own image of what a pro athlete should be. On the one hand, they saw me as a celebrity who had just played in the Super Bowl. They were proud of that, but because of that perceived celebrity status, they didn't think I belonged there. They were all trying to find their balance with how they related to me. Despite that, I went about my business as a full-fledge adult on a mission. As always, I marched to the beat of my own drum, even if that meant I stood out as a peculiar guy.

I went home to New Orleans each weekend to be with Kat in the apartment we were renting. Knowing training camp was right around the corner, I would work out and hang with my family at the house some days. My family loved Kat and they were so excited about the pending arrival of our son. In the weeks leading up to his birth, my mom and sisters hosted a baby shower and made a big fuss over my wife. They were excited to welcome the next generation of Youngs emerging from my generation of six.

On one visit home, Kat complained all day that her back hurt. I rubbed her back a bit and went about my business. That night, I was sleeping like a baby when she startled me, shaking me awake, and said, "Roy, get up. I think it's time." I was midway into a dream, my body was aching from a tough workout earlier that day, and all I wanted to do was rest, but there she was, standing over the bed. "Get up, Roy. My water broke!" It took a few seconds for her words to register in my mind because I thought I was dreaming. Suddenly, my eyes flashed open, and I sat straight up in bed and looked at her. She was leaning over, holding her back. I knew then I wasn't dreaming. This was the real deal.

If there had been a camera on me, the scene playing out would have surely won the prize on *America's Funniest Home Videos*. I was moving as if by remote control as I scampered down the hallway between dream state and half awake. I was in a fog. Eventually, I grabbed my sneakers and put them on my head like a hat. I said, "I'm coming, I'm right behind you!" I walked out of the house with one shoe on and the other one in my hand. I was barely conscious enough to get behind the wheel, but Kat shook me awake so I could drive to the hospital.

By the time we arrived, I was pumped up on adrenaline. I pulled up to the emergency area, where they came out to get her. Then, I parked the car and ran upstairs, and I was in the delivery room in what seemed like less than five minutes. In no time, the baby came out. It was a boy. It all happened so fast I could hardly believe it. Cutting the umbilical cord was a magical moment for me, and watching as they placed my son on my wife's chest was surreal. I was so proud of Kat. I don't think I slept for two days.

While Kat rested in the hospital, I went to the store and got these cigars that had a blue wrapper announcing, "It's a boy!" I passed them out to everybody in the neighborhood, like I used to hand out religious tracts. From my family members to the drug dealers on the corner and even the people at church—everybody I saw got one. I was beaming.

Young family increased from two to three – Roy Jr.

The night we brought Roy Jr. home was special. I wanted to do something symbolic that would consecrate that moment and be a reminder that inside of him was our family lineage, that he had a right and a responsibility to walk in that. The movie *Roots* was still fresh in my mind, and I decided to have a Kunta Kinte and Kizzy kind of experience with my son. I took him outside in the backyard, with Kat following along, and I raised him up to the sky, just like in the movie, and I symbolically gave him back to the ancestors. I consecrated him. The symbolism of it was inspired by *Roots*, but as I held him in the palm of my hand, the entire scene took on a life of its own. He didn't cry as I held him up to the half-moon in the still silence of the night and had a conversation with the Creator. It was peaceful, beautiful.

Being a father was a neat experience, something I felt I was built for. I could not wait to impact my son the way my father had impacted me. I was ready, emotionally, intellectually, and spiritually to be a father, and I thanked God that I was financially ready to invest in his future. It wasn't enough to give him a better life than I'd had. I wanted to be the responsible adult who would positively affect his life and shape his future the same way others had done for me. At that moment, I knew what it meant to shelter your seed from the wrong influences and to expose him to the right ones. I did not want my son to ever feel threatened or insecure. Parenting was intentional for me. I was fully aware and ready for it.

Roy Jr.

Like other new parents, Kat and I had to learn what parenting was about, and we figured it out without causing irreparable damage to our son. We didn't do everything right, but we did our best. In those early years, I learned parenting is not for the faint of heart. It's kind of like changing a flat while the car is still going. I drew on whatever I could grab hold of in my own life to figure it out, always remaining fully aware that the example I set for my son would have a lifelong effect on him. I intended to always have a positive impact on Roy, even if I had to fake it. The superhero I wanted to be for him went far beyond being a football player. Like my dad, I wanted to be both a friend and a disciplinarian, someone he could confide in and trust. I knew a big part of standing up was being authentic, so I couldn't expect anything from him that I wasn't putting out myself. I had to be what I expected him to be, an example not a judge, a role model not a distraction.

Many parents take shortcuts and fool themselves into thinking that giving their kids things is a replacement for the substance of love and parenting. They pacify problems as opposed to addressing them, especially when things get tough. Every kid goes through phases in life, some harder than others. There's the infant and toddler phase, where they're just a little ball of flesh exploring things through taste and touch. Next, they start school and become socialized by their peers. Then, they go through the dreaded adolescent phase, when they lose their minds and go through a temporary insanity. That's not the time to let go; it's the time to bear down and stay engaged. When you do, when they get the love, discipline, caring, and respect they need, kids eventually come back to themselves on the other side (and there is another side). Thankfully, we had years ahead of us before we would experience our version of this.

Back in Philly, Kat, Roy Jr., and I became the three amigos. I loved fatherhood. Roy was a bundle of energy all day, every day. I would come home after a long day at Veteran's Stadium, and he would want to roughhouse as soon as I walked in the door. We had a big living room, and we didn't have much furniture at the time, so for him, that room was a playpen. As soon as I came through the door, he would tackle me, and I would get on my knees and wrestle him. That was his favorite thing. Then, we would put on the boxing gloves and go at it until he was exhausted. Other times, I would come home and put on some New Orleans music because I wanted him to get a flavor of the town where he was born. We would second line dance. I enjoyed watching him hop and slide around trying to mimic me. It was such an innocent time, and crucial because of the formative nature of it. That was love, and I was always happy to give myself over to him.

Sunday after church

The most important thing Kat and I wanted was to raise our son as a responsible, self-respecting, confident, honest human being with integrity. That is not easy to do in this world because there are a lot of distractions along the way, and we ran into them early on. As Roy grew, we placed him in a nursery school at the University of Pennsylvania. There were all these liberal "Pennheads" running the place and they were fascinated with him because of his physical prowess, but I didn't see that as a compliment. It reflected an unconscious bias that Black kids were innately athletic and that's all they had to offer. That offended me and made me suspicious of the school. He was a little kid who could walk on the balance beam like it was nothing. He had more energy than they knew what to do with, but he was more than his physicality. He was an exuberant, intelligent, curious, and energetic kid. That was how I wanted them to view him, not as a physical specimen.

One day, I visited his classroom and I saw him run up to one of the aides and call her by her first name. I motioned for him to come over to me, and I said, "Son, that's *Miss* Amy."

The young white lady politely interrupted and said, "No, that's okay. That's how we all are here." She smiled and hugged Roy like he was her toy.

I said, "No, you don't understand. I want my son to put a handle on your name and any adult he encounters here. All adults are Miss or Ms. or Mister." I stared at her with the firmness of my conviction, and the message was conveyed.

Leaving me with my son, she quickly turned around and walked over to her coworker. They were talking louder than they realized, and I heard the coworker say, "Don't pay him any attention. He's from the South. That's a Southern thing." I thought, *A Southern thing? That's a matter of decency and respect, a common courtesy that, if applied properly, can take him a long way.* I have to admit I was ready to pull him out of that school right then and there. I didn't, but I was a little leery of him going there after that. Thankfully, there were some good people there who had a more positive influence on my son. There was a Black cook in the cafeteria who took a liking to Roy, and they were thick as thieves. He was like an uncle or a grandfather figure for Roy, so that made me feel good.

By then, I was solidly engrossed in my career, but my mind was thinking of the future. I knew I couldn't play football forever, and I didn't want to. Kat and I started kicking around the idea of where we would like to settle in the coming years. Initially, we had a fantasy of buying a brownstone in Harlem, but as the years went on, and we experienced some serious East Coast snowstorms, the Sun Belt began to call to me. "I'm a Southern boy at heart," I told her. I was ready to be closer to the familiarity of home, but I didn't feel I could grow in New Orleans. I thought it might smother me. I was desperately trying to figure out my place in the world. I had done well, up to that point, to stay out of the limelight, the addictive drug that is celebrity and notoriety. The best way I knew to stay clean from that was anonymity. I wanted to stay free from the burden of fame, and I knew I would run up against it if I moved back to New Orleans.

After several discussions and a lot of soul searching, Kat and I decided we would eventually settle in Houston after I retired. We wasted no time finding a house, where she and Roy Jr. lived while I kept things going during football season. They would visit me a few days a week, and those visits were a welcome reprieve from the grinding routine of daily training.

The doorman at the Rittenhouse Square apartments in Philadelphia liked me, and he always loved seeing Kat and Roy when they visited. He would chase Roy around the lobby whenever he rode his Big Wheel, and I think that was a nice break from the routine of his day. Every day, the doorman would open the door, smile, and speak to me. "Good morning, Mr. Young! Great game on Sunday. You really showed them up. Let's do it again this week." I would smile and wave and chat it up with him for a few minutes before heading off to the subway or out for dinner. All of that changed when I started bringing people home with me when I was there alone, which was most of the time. He went from being a friend to pretty much hating me because I "ungentrified" that building over time.

On the way home from the stadium, I would meet different guys, either on the street or on the subway. Most of them were homeless or down on their luck, and we would get into a conversation, usually at my initiation. From time to time, I invited them up to the apartment. The ones who were homeless would get to take a bath, and I would give them a haircut and fix them a hot meal. Each time I walked into the apartment building with a different guy in tow, the doorman turned up his nose and ruffled his brow. It wasn't like I was hanging out in the lobby with these guys or allowing them to run the hallways. I was reaching out in the most authentic way I knew to help my fellow man. Over time, I got a kick out of how the doorman reacted and I just prayed for him.

November is a cold month in Philadelphia. It's not the time to lallygag outside, and the streets are definitely not the place to call home if you can help it. On my typical ride home, I got off at Walnut Street and exited the terminal. One day, I nearly tripped over a homeless guy sleeping on the subway grate. I could tell he was out of it. He was panhandling, and when he asked me for money, something inside told me he needed more. I said, "No, I'm not going to give you the money so you can drink it up."

The look on his face was one of defeat. He scrunched down into his spot, wrapped his thin jacket around his neck, and grumbled something under his breath. "I'll tell you what. I'm gonna call your bluff," I told him. He glanced up at me curiously. Then, I reached my hand down towards his and helped him up. We walked to a nearby IHOP, and I bought him breakfast. The whole walk over, we said very little to each other. He just followed me.

Over breakfast, we talked about his time in the military and some of the horrible things he had seen and done. He was still shaken by it all. Turned out he had been awarded a Bronze Star Medal of valor for his service in the military. Because of his experience in Vietnam, he had suffered trauma, what we call post-traumatic stress disorder, or PTSD, these days, and which was called shell shock back then. That led him to become an alcoholic.

He talked and I listened. Afterward, I said, "Come on, man. I'm going to take you to my place so you can clean up." We walked the few blocks to my apartment building, and as soon as I walked into the lobby, the doorman cut his eyes at me, but he said nothing and neither did I. We walked over to the elevator and took it up to the nineteenth floor, where my apartment was located. I let the guy take a shower. I cut his hair, gave him a shave, and fixed him gumbo and fried chicken. We sat there for hours and just talked. He told me he had a family—a wife, a son, and a daughter. He wanted to be with them, he said, but every time he went home, he couldn't sleep inside. He had to pitch a tent in the back yard. Apparently, his family couldn't deal with that and other strange behaviors he couldn't shake. He did not want to cause them any pain or shame, so he stayed away. I felt empathy for him, and before he left, I prayed with him that he would find peace. He visited me a few more times and began to trust me. With each visit, he was able to clean himself up and have a decent meal.

One day, Matt Darwin, a teammate, and I were walking back to my place when I met up with the same guy. I invited him to come over and hang with Matt and me. That was one of the most memorable days of my life. Matt and I literally led that guy to Christ. We prayed the prayer of salvation and he accepted Christ. It was beautiful and he cried, not in a regular way, but almost like he was cleansing himself. We let him get it all out. After that encounter, we would meet up from time to time and sit, eat, pray, and study. I did not know it at the time, but I was mentoring him in a sense.

Two months later, Matt and I ended up in Pottstown, Pennsylvania, on a Little League field. The guy had invited us to watch his kids play ball. That day, after the game, he confessed that months earlier he had committed a petty crime, shoplifting. I told him, "You can't get a fresh start until you face your past, man. You'll never be able to embrace full citizenship or your full personhood with that on your back. If you really want to get your life together, you've got to get all that stuff behind you." That was the last time I saw him. For months, I wondered what became of him, until one day I got a letter from him in prison. He had turned himself in for his crime. By then, he had a few months to serve until he was released. He had been working on his college degree in prison, reconnecting with his family, and putting his past behind him. He thanked me for encouraging him to get his life together, and I was blessed to know he had done the right thing.

That encounter led me to a multitude of other events that connected me to the real Philadelphia and fueled within me an intrinsic call to service. I went through a myriad of things to satisfy my growing desire to serve others, from organizing a youth football camp to feeding homeless youth. It was a random assortment of activities focused on young people that began to mold into service. Interestingly, the NFL's efforts at community outreach with groups like the United Way were also available to me, but that never fed my need because it didn't touch the kind of people I wanted to reach, the outcast and marginalized knuckleheads who were like me. I wanted to get into the nitty-gritty aspects of service and interact with them. It was like looking in a mirror. I saw me in them, and just like I found my way to wake up, clean up, and stand up, I wanted to help them do the same.

Gradually, doors began to open for one opportunity after another, and I investigated them all. I had no plan or blueprint. I was just going without knowing. I did not know why I was going in that direction or seeking to be anonymous while doing it. None of that was intentional. Unbeknownst to me, those experiences would become prophetic for the direction my life would take. In my silence, I had an internal conversation about what it all meant. I was curious and confused about this growing desire for service, this drive developing within me. At the same time, my enthusiasm and enjoyment of the thing I had dreamed of and longed for was drying up, and that alarmed me. I couldn't even tell Kat what I had been thinking because my career, at that point, was our ticket to a comfortable future.

My last year and a half in the NFL was a blur. Each day, each practice, each game, I found myself practically sleepwalking through it. At that point, it was just a job that allowed me to feed my family and prepare for our future. I was grateful to be in that position, but I did not have the passion to do it anymore. Nearly eight years in, I had lost my love and excitement for the game, and that was a dangerous place for me to be. I felt like I was living a dual life. On the one hand, I was discovering a deep desire and appreciation for serving people. On the other hand, I had this physically demanding job that didn't feed my soul. These sides of me were colliding, and I couldn't fake it much longer. I felt like a fugitive whenever I was in the locker room or out on the field, like I was running from something. When I went to Houston to spend time with my family or whenever I reached out to serve the community, I felt like I was running towards something. It was a strange dichotomy that caused me to have a gut feeling that the end was near.

Be Ready for What's Next

Standing up is about being your authentic self, not a phony version of who you think others want to see, not something you fake your way through just to win favor with someone else. When you stand up, you unleash the true essence of who you are. That is what people are drawn to, and that is what fuels your desires, your thoughts, and your actions. You might not know the full picture of the Creator's purpose for your life, but you know you're being positioned to walk in something bigger than you can fully comprehend.

Being in that place is invigorating and intimidating at the same time. You are excited about this new you, and you want to live it out in its fullness. You're also a little nervous that you won't be able to stand up at every opportunity. That is when you know you have to trust the Creator because, no matter the circumstance, now that you have journeyed through wake up, clean up, and stand up, you are ready to show up.

When it's time to show up, you become more aware of your surroundings—the people, distractions, activities, and signals, all designed to teach you something. Just like with cleaning up, your stand up is perpetual. You're continuously doing the work to show up, and even though you fear messing up or acting for self-gain, you know in your heart that this life thing is not only about you. The people who matter most are the true recipients when you show up.

The self-discipline you have learned thus far on your journey has now matured and magnified. You proudly exude your authentic self and carry out your mission. Now is your chance to show up.

Photo Gallery

Mother (Joyce Young), General Manager (Jim Murray), Father (Wallace Young), Wife (Kathleen Young), and me (Roynell Young). First trip to Philadelphia right after NFL draft

High school football   *College football*

College football

Pro football

Roy Jr.

Top: Unenlightened days   Top: Family Easter photo with siblings circa 1965
Bottom: Venice Beach with Brenard Wilson   Bottom: Siblings

Eric, Kathleen, and Roy   Together at senior sports banquet

SHOW UP STRONG

"If you never show up, you never know what could have been." ~Coach Roynell Young

Summers spent at my Grandma Gibbs's house in Thibodeaux, Louisiana were the best. These days, people visit this southwest section of the state to experience a swamp tour, pet an alligator, or go fishing. For me, back then, life was all about having fun and playing near Bayou Lafourche in the noonday heat. Just about the time I would be having the most fun with my cousins and some of the neighborhood kids, my grandma would call us in to eat lunch and take a nap. "Dang, there she goes again," I'd mumble under my breath. I would get so upset with her because she seemed to always choose the time when things were getting really fun for us. "Doesn't this old lady know I'm in the middle of having the most fun I've ever had playing with my friends?" Again, this was the conversation going on inside my head. I would never have spoken those words aloud for anyone to hear, especially not her. In the heat of my frustration, I would continue my huffing and puffing. "I'm ten years old. I'm a grown man. You can't tell me what to do." Little did I know with my decade of wisdom that, left to my own devices, I would play until I dropped from a heatstroke. I didn't understand that my grandma was protecting me from the elements and, more importantly, from myself. Her experience had taught her something valuable that I had yet to learn. Wisdom and knowledge are mostly born from experience.

By the time you show up, you exhibit a level of confidence and wisdom based on your life experiences. You might not even realize it, but others notice it. They see something different in you. Usually, they cannot quite put their finger on it, but they know something is different. It's all the result of what you've experienced, and you cannot rush the wisdom gained from experience. You do not accumulate wisdom overnight. When you are observant, life teaches its lessons in the most unexpected ways and sometimes through the most mundane means.

Showing up allows you to put into practice the lessons learned from the experiences of waking up, cleaning up, and standing up. Whenever I have been obedient, studious, and humble enough to pay attention and listen to the voice of the Creator, I've been tremendously blessed by it. Showing up is being in the moment and knowing you are connected to what you were created to do. Being in the moment allows you to free yourself from the pressure to figure out your next move. You still need that skill once you show up because now you are living in the essence of your purpose. Now, you are able to sit back, relax, and enjoy the moment, any moment, every moment.

A New Direction in Life

Everything I have done in my life has become a guidepost for what's next. I have done so many things that I've forgotten half of them, even though I've gotten great satisfaction from doing them. To have called attention to those activities for sheer acknowledgment would have ruined the moment. That's why I don't like accolades. When I am in the moment, I want to be right there, doing my best, not performing to earn a trophy. Don't get me wrong. I appreciate acknowledgment, but I don't need it to know that what I have done is good and fulfills my purpose.

At this stage of my life, every action is all about service. Seeing the result of someone's life being changed for the better is what gets me going. The awards and accolades are nice, but I have to buffer myself to make sure they don't become my reason for doing what I do. My aim is to please my Creator through service to others, not to please other people so they will stroke my ego or tell others how big and bad I am. If that were my motivation, I would not be where I am today. I have been a passenger on that ride, and I voluntarily hopped off. It was one of the best decisions I ever made.

I probably knew two years before my NFL career ended that it was time to call it quits. Life as I knew it changed around 1987. I was coming of age and coming into my own as a human, as a man, as a father, as a husband. I had become a seasoned NFL player, and I was pleased with the evolution of my skill and my career. Inevitably, I started to consider what was next for me and my family, and how much longer football would be a part of my life. Giving myself the space to think and question my motives and my future allowed the transition to happen naturally, organically, easily, to the point that I felt no pain or regret about it.

I would have these conversations inside my head: "I'm not sure how much longer I can do this. I have to stack my chips and reserve as much as I can for my family and our future. I'm getting to the point that I no longer get pleasure out of doing this, but for now, I'll hang on until I figure out what I want to do next." Each time these conversations happened in my mind, I leaned into them and then shook them off because to ruminate over them was dangerous for me. Professional athletes are trained to be myopic. They are trained to have tunnel vision, to focus on a single thing—winning. That is intentional, and it serves to keep the revenue rolling in for the teams and the leagues. It also helps keep players focused to reduce injuries. So I told myself, "You can't let these thoughts consume you, or else you will get killed on the field!"

My career came to a sudden and satisfying head after the infamous Fog Bowl in December of 1988, when we played the Chicago Bears in Soldier Field. The fog was so thick that day no one could see the game on TV. Even on the field, the density of the fog was something I had never seen. I couldn't see my hand in front of my face. Consequently, there was a lot of stuff happening on that field that no one but the players, the umpires, and the coaches knew. Guys were settling old scores left and right, and it was getting ugly. It was like a game of Mortal Kombat. The quarterback couldn't see the receivers, so it became a running game with fierce, hard tackles.

During a time out, I ran over to the sidelines for a drink and thought, *My hand feels weird*. That's when I noticed my teammates pointing at my hand in shock. The ring finger on my left hand had snapped practically in half and was dangling by the skin. With the extreme cold and dampness, I didn't even feel it. I vaguely remembered the play—a hard hit to a receiver who was coming off the line. I had stopped him, grabbed his jersey, and flung him to one side. My finger went right along with him, ripping the ligaments. It was so violent and quick that I didn't think anything of it. I just kept playing. With the final quarter left to play, I taped that ring finger to the pinky finger to get some stability and got back in the game. Afterward, I needed surgery and had to get a pin put in it.

At the close of that game, I had an epiphany. Usually, I would run into the locker room after the game, but when that game was over, I stood in the middle of Soldier Field and looked up at the sky. I said to myself in a quiet voice, "I'm finished. I'm finished. I'm finished." I had played my last game and I knew it was over. I was at peace. It was kind of like in the movie *Forrest Gump* when Forrest is running across the country and all these groupies are following him. Suddenly, he stops, and the whole crowd screeches to a halt behind him. They think he has

155

something profound to say. They're mesmerized by him because they have built him up to prophet status. He finally says, "I'm tired. I think I'll go home. I don't want to do this anymore." That was my moment in the stadium. I didn't want to do it anymore. Essentially, that feeling was a foreshadowing of things to come.

When I got the call from Buddy Ryan in 1989, I was at my home in Houston, recovering from knee surgery, so I wasn't working out in earnest. I was just trying to get my knee well.

"Hey, Old Pro," that was his nickname for me. "The money men upstairs are going in a different direction next season." I could hear it coming. His words were almost an echo, a confirmation of a feeling I had deep inside. "They want young guys, fresh meat, and you're not a part of that." He was matter of fact, straight to the point. "It's been a pleasure, Young. I just wanted to call you personally because, next time I see you, I want to be able to look you in the eyes." I could tell it was a tough call for him, but I appreciated his candor.

I said, "Coach, I appreciate that. All I ask of you is that you treat me like a man." I told him it had been a pleasure to be on the team for the past nine years.

"Good then," he said. "Maybe we can sit down someday soon and have a cup of coffee." Then, he hung up.

Although I felt a tinge of anxiety about what was next for me, the call was almost a welcome relief. Almost. After I hung up and breathed a deep exhale, I realized something. I had just had surgery to reset my torn and broken finger and my knee injury from the Fog Bowl. There I was, recovering, doing physical therapy, and training as best I could to get myself back up to speed to play again, and now I was cut from the team. It was kind of cold, but that's life in the NFL.

Kathleen comforted me the best she could. She was wise enough and skilled enough to know I needed encouragement and some time to think through our next move. I knew she would be one hundred percent with me, no matter what. We had to chart a new direction for our family, and it felt good to know I had a good woman with me every step of the way. We had lived a pretty frugal lifestyle and needed to kick our future plans into gear right away to make sure Roy Jr.'s life wasn't interrupted. Initially, even though I felt I was pursuing my purpose, I had the feeling of being totally lost. I didn't know what to do next. Career counseling was available to me, but I figured my faith was my coach, so in the peace of solitude, I began to piece together what was next for me and my family.

Meanwhile, the NFL and the Eagles wanted to turn my departure into a public relations story. I had been the last starter on the Super Bowl team to be let go, so the news was handled pretty delicately. The Eagles wanted me to fly to Philadelphia for a press conference, but I didn't see how that would benefit me for the next step of my life, so I instructed them to go ahead without me and spin the story any way they wanted. I had shut that door and I was at peace with it. When the news reached my family, they were all supportive of me. Best of all, my mom sent me the most beautiful, tender letter expressing a lifetime of her love for her children and her pride in all of us turning out to be good human beings. She mentioned how proud she was of me and mentioned she was thankful that I had never done anything to damage the family name. That letter touched me deep in my soul. Knowing she was proud of the man I had become meant the world to me.

"Showing up means unleashing your better angels."
~Coach Roynell Young

As I reflected on my life in search of the meaning of everything I had experienced up to that point, my focus shifted, and the mosaic of the future slowly began to come together. Now that I was free from the rigor of my athletic career, I had time to pursue a new direction for my life. Even though the safety blanket of the NFL had been taken away from me, the door was now open for growth in other areas that would have taken longer to explore had I continued to lean on the crutch of the NFL. I wasn't exactly sure what was next for me, but I was excited about serving people to help better their lives, which was fine, but I still needed to bring in some dollars. Pro athletes didn't earn the millions back then that they do now. The compensation packages were a far cry from what agents negotiate for players these days, so I knew I had to get started with something immediately.

A new business opportunity presented itself to me, and I jumped at it. I became an insurance broker and started building my business. I had no compelling reason for choosing insurance, but in no time, I became successful at it. I felt like I was back in the wilderness, trying to figure out life all over again, only this time, I had some life experiences and wisdom to guide me. Later, I realized that selling insurance made sense because it had to do with service to others. That was where my heart was. I wanted to do something that had a service element to it. In my mind, that was the bridge for me to meet people from different backgrounds and provide them a service to help protect their family, but first, I had to make sure my own house was in order.

Showing Up for My Son

Over the years, I watched Roy go through all the ups and downs, the successes and failures that most kids go through. He was a good kid who made Kat and me proud. If I was the play buddy for Roy, Kat was his confidant. Over the years, those two grew so close that he would tell her just about everything going on with him. If he was having problems with the kids or teachers at school, he told his mom. If he had an ache or pain, he told her. As he grew up, he would only come to me if the problem was a life-or-death matter in his mind, the last inning, with no other options. Thankfully, there were not many of those.

When he came to her about his dating woes, Kat would ask him, "Why don't you go talk to your dad about that?" However, Roy would decline, figuring he would only come to me if there were no other options. My feelings were never hurt by it. I liked the fact that Kat and Roy always had a special bond. They still do. When he was a teenager, I would tell him, "Don't come to me with that lightweight stuff because I'm not going to tell you what you want to hear. I'm gonna give it to you straight." So he knew he would get the unadulterated truth from me, even if it hurt his feelings. Despite that, or maybe because of it, my son looked up to me. That warms my heart; it would for any father. My sole desire, as it relates to him, was to never do anything to disappoint him. Throughout his high school years, we dealt with girls and sports and grades, and all of that. I enjoyed it all.

Roy Jr. is my namesake and I want him to always be proud of who he is named for. However, I've had some regrets over the years about naming him after me. I don't know if I did it out of arrogance or laziness or if it was just presumptuous, but I wish I would have given him more breadth and space to establish his own identity with a different name. I understand why men do it. Honestly, I think it's driven by ego. Looking back on it now, with my clarity and maturity, I know the Creator gives us our own unique place in this world. It was selfish and unfair of me to put the weight of my shadow on my son's shoulders.

At the same time, from the standpoint of creating or continuing a legacy, I respect what the ancestors have done over generations with naming patterns. Names connect us. After all, I am named for my Uncle Nick, whose real name is Roynell. He's a big part of why I was able to clean up and stand up. I have always been proud to carry his name because I have always admired him. I hope my son can say the same for me. He handles it well. In fact, I think he loves his name now. He's proud of it, but if I had it to do over again, I would choose his name with less ego and more thoughtfulness.

One key figure in the parable of the prodigal son is as critical to the story as the son himself—the father. When my experience as the father of the prodigal son was played out, my son didn't decide to leave home to find himself. Instead, I sent him away. It was the hardest thing I have ever done. Sending my son out was a scary move, but it was necessary for his growth and character development. It was necessary for me to stand up for him and show up with a tough love to guide him in finding his way back to himself.

During his first year in college, Roy wasn't focused even though I'd fully laid out the objectives for him to meet. "Everyone has a role in this family," I said. "You have an obligation to go to school, keep your grades up, and graduate. You signed off on this, and I expect you to follow through." His first year at New Mexico Military Institute proved to me that he was unfocused and immature. He didn't take his coursework or what I had told him seriously. He had been accepted there on a basketball scholarship, but Kat and I knew when he went away that he was a bit immature, mainly because we had sheltered him from a lot of things. During his first year, he connected with a bunch of fast-talking guys, there from New York City, and he got distracted. His grades suffered, so he decided he would go to summer school to make up for it. Instead, I brought him home and forced him to come up with an alternate plan before the next school year started.

"Everything in this house has a purpose; that includes you," I told him. "Your mother and I, we both have a purpose, and we know what that is. You have to figure out what yours is, and until you do, you're going to feel like an outsider in this family." I wasn't kicking him out of the house or out of the family. I was forcing him to connect with his purpose for the first time in his life. I had consecrated him to the ancestors all those years ago, and I was not about to watch my expectations of him go down the drain. I gave him a week to come up with something. During that time, Kat and I talked about alternatives and decided that, whatever happened, we had to agree and be on the same page. We had to present a united front. To say we had some intense discussions is putting it lightly.

After a week of hanging with his friend Sterling Jackson, Roy came home. I sat down at the kitchen table with him and pulled out a stack of pamphlets, one from each branch of the military. "This is my plan," I said. "Since you don't know how you'll contribute to make this family whole, you can choose one of these options." He was speechless.

The next day, I took him downtown to the U.S. Customs House, the same place where Muhammad Ali refused to be inducted into the army. The entire scene was strange, unsettling, and disruptive to the structure of our family. He'd had his chance to wake up and stand up, but he had refused, so I had to do it for him. That day, he elected to enter the United States Navy. With the papers signed, Roy and I returned home to find his bedroom completely redesigned.

"Where's my room?" he asked. In the week he was away trying to determine his next steps, I had made some decisions. His bed was gone, the clothes in his closet were missing, and all his electronics were boxed up.

I said, "That's not your room anymore; it's my office now. You're a guest at this house from this point forward. There's a sleeping bag in the closet. You can sleep in the guest room." He walked away with tears in his eyes.

In the weeks leading to his departure, there was a lot of tension in our house. The three of us spoke very few words to each other. Even Kat and I remained mostly silent towards one another for fear of saying the wrong thing or simply falling apart emotionally. I couldn't sleep for days because I had begun to second-guess my decision. I did not want to punish Roy, but I knew something had to be done to help him find himself. I was raising a man, someone who would be independent and self-sufficient. Even though this was an extreme move, I had to keep telling myself it was the best thing for him. After Kat and I dropped him off for his induction ceremony, we returned home in silence. That was the most difficult thing I'd ever done in my life. I think I cried harder than she did that night.

At the close of his basic training, Roy wrote Kat and me a letter. In it, he apologized for not being the son we had raised him to be. He thanked us for forcing him to discover a path for his life, and he told us we were the best parents he could ever ask for. We were extremely grateful to read those words because it told us that we had, in fact, done the right thing. While we could breathe a sigh of relief knowing he was finally coming to himself, that breather was, unfortunately, temporary.

Just as Roy was cruising along, becoming an adult, and standing up as a medic in the navy, the war in Afghanistan broke out and the marine infantry group he was attached to was sent to the Middle East. Our hearts dropped and it took every ounce of faith we had not to fall apart. We followed the news of the war and communicated with him as often as we could via emails and the occasional call when he could find the time. Those calls were our lifeline to our one and only son. Never would we have wished he would experience the things he did while there, but like the prodigal son's father, I had to bear the burden of my decision to let my son go and pray he would return whole. Thankfully, he did return home and professed himself better for all that he had been through.

In a sense, the prodigal son had become a cautionary tale for my son and me. When I sent Roy away, I did not send him away as an object of scorn. I sent him away to help him realize he comes from the bloodline of people who came to this land in the bottom of a ship. Those people were so strong that they held on and held out. I have to believe they were hoping someone later in their bloodline would experience justice they could only dream of. Knowing that, I had the responsibility to teach my son that someone in his long-ago ancestry envisioned their descendants rising to a life worthy of everything they had sacrificed for us to have.

I loved my son so much that I wasn't going to allow the external influences to produce something counter to his best interests. My decision is not the answer for everyone, but I knew Roy had greatness deep down inside of him, yet he had decided to coast through life by doing just enough to get by. I knew that kind of attitude wouldn't serve him well in life, so I had to do something extreme to arrest his thinking and grab his attention. I wasn't raising a boy; I was raising a man, and he had to learn from experience how to get through life as an adult. Part of my job as a parent was to allow him the gift of struggle so he could show up strong.

Without struggle, young people think they are entitled to every good thing that comes their way and that every bad thing is someone else's fault. Sometimes, kids want a barrier-free life, but all that does is cause them to be self-weakened. Struggle builds character. Although parents do not want their kids to suffer, those who take the "school of hard knocks" approach to child rearing do want their kids to struggle, to figure things out.

Much of my generation stripped the struggle from our kids. We thought we were helping them by taking away the gift of struggle. Instead, we stifled their growth.

Struggle is an essential tool that helps young people endure. When parents fail to give their kids the chance to exercise those muscles, they rob kids of the gift of struggle and render them helpless in many ways. Without struggle, kids do not develop, they do not grow. They atrophy. Parents do a disservice to their kids when they serve up all life's experiences to them on a platter with a cherry on top rather than allow them some difficult experiences so they will have depth and substance. Everyone has to go through something in life to be well balanced and to appreciate God's gifts.

Showing Up for Myself

My insurance business was going along pretty well when I started hearing talk about bringing me back to the NFL. A few months had passed since I was let go, and I'd had conversations with some of my former teammates. "No, man, it's not over, you're not done," they said. It's funny when you know it's over and the time has come to move on, but other people are still holding on, hoping to get one more big performance out of you. It feels good that they still believe in you, but what matters more are your goals and desires for your own life. However, I took my eyes off the prize for a moment. I gave in and got a couple of try-outs through Coach Dick Vermeil.

I went to San Francisco to check out the 49ers. While I was there, Coach Ray Rhodes was giving Jerry Rice a hard time, using me as a source of motivation to egg him on, saying, "Yeah, I've got somebody in here to challenge you today, Jerry!" I could see the apprehension on Rice's face because he knew me from when I was on top of my game. It felt good to know my reputation still held some weight. There I was, out on the field just a few months after having knee surgery, dragging my leg. In my mind, the last thing I wanted to do was tangle with Jerry Rice.

I ran some one-on-one routes with a third-string backup receiver, and I had to admit to myself that I looked awful. Heck, I felt awful. I didn't have the speed or the moves I'd had all those years playing for the Eagles. As much as the guys on the 49ers chuckled at how that receiver struggled to keep up with me, I figured they probably also got a good laugh watching me, an all-but-washed-up player, try to defend routes like I was a rookie. The late great Bill Walsh came up to me after drills and shook my hand, and then he said, "Roynell, it's a pleasure to meet you. You were a great player in this league."

I noted the operative word, "were." That was further confirmation that it was over for me, but with one more last-chance opportunity waved before my face, I left there and went to Minnesota. Before they put me on the field to run drills, I had to get checked out by the doctor, and thanks to my busted knee, I failed the physical. That was when I said my final farewell. With those two last-ditch efforts, I had gotten it out of my system. My football career was officially over.

Transitioning from a career—any career—can be hard. As a former football player, it was especially difficult. Even though I never cared for the fame of it all, once that was gone, I realized the gaping hole it left in my life. I never wanted the trappings of fame—being recognized everywhere I went, people asking for my autograph, strangers giving me things just because I was an athlete, and other special treatment—but in the back of my mind, I liked knowing those things were there for me to experience anytime I wanted. The more time that separated me from my life as an athlete, the more withdrawn I became. It was hard.

I realized in hindsight that not taking advantage of the career counseling offered by the NFL was a mistake. I have learned that the bigger picture is called that because when you're in the midst of a crisis or a transition, all you see is what you see. You cannot see what else is there, the bigger picture. Others know, and that's why they offer to help. To refuse that help reveals your ego, your false bravado, your stupidity. Because of that, I felt stuck. Being stuck was real and it was intense, but it was temporary. I had to come back to myself and remember that I'm a fighter. I do not believe in self-pity, so I had no choice but to find a way to keep moving.

Looking back on my experiences, my drive to serve always centered around the development of children. Driving around Houston, selling insurance products, I would see kids of all ages hanging out at various times of the day. They were school age, but they were not in school. I could tell most of them either had nothing more to look forward to than hanging out on the corner, or they were waiting for the opportunity to get into some trouble. Either way, my heart went out to them and I knew there was more for these kids.

Matt Darwin, my former teammate, retired a few years after I did and we would meet me at the gym to work out together. He was an upright, moral, stand-up kind of guy who had been a great influence in my life while playing for the Eagles, and he was with me when I led the Vietnam vet to Christ. Over the years, we had remained tight. We both wanted to make a big impact on our community off the field, something that would help the next generation. We wanted to impact kids the way Jesus showed his disciples, by tossing a wide net and pulling in as many as we could. Our version of that was going to shopping malls, hanging out, and seeing what we could come up with to help kids. Within a few Saturdays, however, I killed that idea. "Matt, look at us," I said. "We're two grown men, hanging out in the malls trying to engage kids. This doesn't look right. It's creepy. This is not the entry point." So I went back to the drawing board.

While building my insurance business, I started hanging out with a guy I met at church, Mike Anderson. I liked him a lot. He was charismatic and had a commanding presence, and he was thoughtful. Mike had a startup advertising consulting business he was trying to get off the ground. The entrepreneur spirit in us connected with a common passion for developing young people. I later learned he was a youth pastor at a church I had been attending. Sometimes, amazing things happen when you put your own needs on the shelf to help others.

Over the weeks, our conversations turned to the needs of kids—what was happening in the community, what was missing that kids desperately needed, what organizations existed to help, and how effective (or not) they were at inspiring kids to do and be more. We came to the conclusion that the problem with our youth wasn't limited to the kids alone. There was an ecosystem surrounding them that contributed to the demise we observed.

Parents and grandparents played a role in the development of these kids we saw hanging out. So did their nutrition and fitness. Their experiences in school and the education system's ability to meet kids where they were and take them beyond their current situation, or the lack thereof, was a key determinant in their success. The housing and surrounding areas where kids lived helped shape their view of themselves and the world. Mike and I discussed all this and came up with what, in our minds, were some pretty impressive solutions to help kids succeed. Problem was we were just two guys talking. We had ideas but no game plan and no concrete program to make anything happen.

One day, Mike and I got in my truck and drove around Houston, still dreaming out loud and talking to anyone who would listen and who we thought would support the idea. We passed through Fifth Ward and Third Ward and witnessed all sorts of nefarious activities. We talked more about what we would do if we had the resources. What if we had some land and a staff and other adults who cared? Then, we rode up on Sunnyside, and that's when we saw it, the disturbing sight of kids without any adult supervision. They were hanging out on the street corner like a pack of wolves. We observed drug sales going down, fights, shootings, and all kinds of other activities. "Surely, there are groups out here trying to address this," Mike said. We agreed that there were organizations in the neighborhood, but obviously they weren't getting to the core of what we witnessed. After that day, we began reaching out to pastors at the local churches.

Everyone had a pessimistic view of the situation. More than one pastor told us the problem was just too big for their organization to solve. The more we heard that, the more we felt we had to step into the gap and do something. We were getting all psyched up about doing something big to make a difference. The youth outreach at church began to grow beyond the church walls and turned into a 911 call in the African American community in terms of helping kids with their immediate needs. Mike and I realized the cry in the community was beyond the church and that a larger swath of kids desperately needed what we were putting in place. Our desire was to create something that had a more positive impact beyond the church walls. To do that, we needed a structure to transfer information, culturally and academically, to help the kids understand the fullness of who they were.

I wanted to define myself separate from football. I was ready to close that door and open other doors to begin a new direction in life. Better days were ahead personally and professionally. Still, I had a recurring dream that I was back on the field. In my waking time, I felt confused some days about my expectations for the future. There were times when I'd feel the urge to go back to the NFL. In my subconscious mind, the thought of it was like a limb had been severed, but I still felt the sensation of it being there. It was weird. Consciously, I had not only closed the door, but I had also locked it and I had no desire or intention to return. I did not want to be like Lot's wife in the Bible, looking back on what I had left behind and ending up turning into a pillar of salt. I was so close to finally making peace with my NFL career being over.

Just as I felt I had some clarity for what was next for me, my former agent called to say Tampa Bay was having difficulty with their first-round draft choice. He was a rookie. The team leadership was nervous and wanted a veteran to step in because they didn't know if this guy would fizzle out. They needed some insurance, so they wanted me to come out to consider a spot on the team. By then, I had almost completely released football as a possibility for my future. I was done, or so I thought. When I told him as much, the agent didn't believe me. "They're going to guarantee you a bonus. Man, you can't pass this up." I laughed because I knew I actually could pass it up. So I laid out my demands, the specifics of what I'd need before even considering a deal. I demanded a bunch of stuff I knew they wouldn't agree to. Truth be told, I was being unreasonable because I didn't have the courage to say, "I don't want to do this."

During the negotiations, the management at Tampa Bay invited me to come out. They were willing to consider everything, within reason, but they wanted to see me in person. With just one more week of training camp, they needed somebody in a hurry. Knowing I had the upper hand, I advised my agent to tell the team's general manager that I wanted twenty-four hours to think about it. When I was in the NFL, there's no way I would have pushed the envelope like that. With guys at all levels of talent clamoring to get into the league, you just did not negotiate. You could push the envelope a bit, but not too much.

It was a different game back then, but this was now, and I was me. I had been through a lot, and here I was, showing up strong, certain I could take the deal or leave it and be fine either way, but I would not settle. I had options, slim as they were. I knew I did not have to go back to football in a lowly state. Still, I had to decide. That was the longest twenty-four hours I had ever experienced. I stayed up all night, didn't sleep, could not focus. Minutes passed by like hours and hours went by like days. I wrestled and prayed and reasoned with God. By the next morning, I had come to a decision. I would take the deal.

The idea of getting back on the field wasn't the driving force behind my decision. Neither was the money. My mind was still focused on serving kids and making a difference in communities, so I rationalized that football would be a great platform to do that. I could not ignore the moral erosion I saw as a fundamental threat causing young men to lose direction and become lost. They were so full of energy as they approached the peak of their strength, yet they were fighting the wrong battles and losing because of lack of direction. Young people should be the vanguard of the future, but they were living their lives in a toxic and counterproductive way. I reasoned that, with this new opportunity, I could network with other players, use the NFL to get publicity for what I was doing, and grow the organization into something bigger than what I could do on my own. It would be great.

When I called to accept the offer, I had butterflies in my stomach, which was weird. On the call were my agent and the general manager of the team. We skipped the pleasantries, and the GM got straight to the point.

"Well, Young, what's it gonna be? We're ready to sign you. Are you ready to take the deal?"

I could hear the agent breathing on the line. He was ready. This would be a big payday for him. Heck, it would be a big payday for me too. All the hours I had spent thinking about this moment suddenly collapsed into a tiny pin drop. I opened my mouth to say, "I'll take it," but what came out instead was, "Nah, I'ma pass on this one, man." Something had taken over my brain and would not let the words come out of my mouth the way I had rehearsed them. In fact, as I responded, I began smacking the palm of my hand against my forehead. Inside my head, I heard, *"Shut up! You're blowing it!"* I was having an out-of-body experience. It was strange. I took a deep breath, exhaled hard, and said, "I respect you, and I respect your team, but I'm not willing to run through brick walls like I did as a rookie. I'm a father and a husband, and it's time for me to grow up. Thanks, but no thanks."

The agent jumped into the conversation and tried to get me to clarify what I meant. He asked if I was sure, and I said yes. He was stunned, baffled, nearly speechless. I said, "Listen, I realize this is a great opportunity, but I don't want any part of this anymore." He grunted and huffed, and I could tell he was biting his lip in an effort to keep from yelling at me. He kept his cool and so did I, but deep inside I still had a tinge of doubt. What had I just done? Had I blown my last opportunity to do something big in the NFL, to redeem myself as a great player, or even to use my celebrity status to build a future for others, like I was planning? The GM thanked me and told me he respected my decision. I exhaled, hung up, and leaned back into the chair.

When I got off the phone, I felt like the weight of the world had been lifted from my shoulders. Somehow, making that decision freed my mind and allowed me to move forward with my plans to create my dream, an organization to uplift and encourage young people, to offer them knowledge, resources, and hope. Eventually, that idea became my sole focus. My interest in insurance faded and my attention turned one hundred percent towards building this dream. Once I put my heart and soul into it, I didn't look back. I had shut the door to my former life and embraced the cloak of anonymity. As we got the organization off the ground, nobody involved knew I was a former football player, except Mike, and I swore him to secrecy. None of that mattered. More important than my former life was getting the people in my new circle of influence to understand what I already knew, which is that whatever we needed already existed.

Unearthing what God has already put here on this earth requires discipline. It does not require some extraordinary charisma, notoriety, or ambition. You do not need celebrity power or some fancy strategic plan. What is required is a heart for service. Sometimes, to live out your purpose, you just need to first show up.

LIVING OUT
MY PURPOSE

"I would unite with anybody to do right and with nobody to do wrong." ~Frederick Douglass

By our tenth anniversary, Kathleen and I had learned to embrace delayed gratification, especially when it came to material things. We focused on saving rather than buying things to look flashy. Plus, we had both come from humble beginnings, so we didn't need all the fancy stuff to make us happy. We were glad to have taken that approach to life because we were about to begin a journey where that nest egg we'd built would be our sole income. That money had to cover our living expenses. Later, some of it was used to launch the organization I believed was the epitome of me living out my true purpose.

Playing in the NFL had afforded me the opportunity to transition into a comfortable middle-class lifestyle, but that collided with my newfound revelation of service. The transformation I was experiencing caused me to view the ideal that is the American Dream through the lens of the community I was serving. I was grateful to have had my prodigal-son experience—to have come into this world part of a good family, lost myself in the temptations of life, weathered the storms that resulted from my foolish escapades, and found myself again. Not only had I enjoyed a dream career, but I had hit the lottery with finding my partner for life and creating the next generation to continue our legacy. Now, I had reached this next leg of the journey, and I found myself in conflict with a lot of long-held beliefs.

Kat and I did the social scene, participating in Jack & Jill, the Links, and other organizations designed to uplift the best and brightest among us. But I was disturbed by the dichotomy between that scene and what I was seeing with the kids we had begun to help through our organization. I could live safely in the cocoon we had created and look out for me and mine, or I could discover something more to do with the time I have here on Earth.

As I tried to reconcile the two realities my life bordered, my conversation began to change. Kat and I would attend dinner parties and other events with the local elites, and my new conversation about community development and helping the less fortunate seemed repulsive to some of those I spoke with. That segment of the population, which had previously gravitated to me, was suddenly disinterested in what I had to say. My intention was to put out a clarion call to those I thought would be interested in helping, not only for the sake of the community, but for the sake of their own children. I had the foresight to know that, at some point, my son—and their children, too—would either interact with the kids in less desirable neighborhoods or our kids would be treated like those kids through no fault of their own.

A new stream of consciousness was developing within me, not in terms of legacy, but in terms of my marching orders to fulfill my purpose. The questions that drove me day after day were: Is just being a good person and having a family enough? What about the community that surrounds you, the people, and their needs? What's the point in having everything when those around you are in need? The people I was serving were in survival mode, and as such, did not have the privilege of living the American Dream. I wanted to change that, and I was determined to do it with or without the support of those in power and privileged positions.

The concept Mike Anderson and I were developing seemed to fit well within the church environment. After all, Mike was a youth minister and the principles we were teaching fell in line with biblical principles. Unfortunately, we got pushback from some churches and the cold shoulder from others, so we abandoned that collaboration idea and instead looked to partner with community groups. Even that proved to be an uphill battle. By then, my appetite for service was growing and I was anxious to make a difference. Mike and I decided we would just go where the kids were, so we found ourselves meeting up at a school and shooting hoops on the basketball court on Saturday mornings. We'd use the time to brainstorm and plot our next moves. One day, we hung around longer than usual and three brash kids approached us, talking trash.

"Hey, man, what are you doing on our court? This is our 'hood."

Mike and I looked at each other, surprised at the boldness of these kids. Just as Mike was about to roll up his sleeves and give them a lesson in respecting your elders, I nudged him and said, "No, let's play along. This might be an opening for us." He looked surprised, but agreed to follow along with me.

I walked up to the kid who was doing the most talking and said, "If you guys are that cold-blooded, let's put something on it." Then, the whole bunch of them started whining about how they didn't have any money to bet on a game against us. That was no surprise, so I took things a step further. "I'll tell you what, you see that pizza place across the street. We'll play two out of three games. If you guys beat us, we'll buy all the pizza and soda you can handle. Just give us two hours so we can talk to you."

Once they agreed to our deal, it was game on. I was fresh out of the NFL, so I was still in tip-top shape. Mike, on the other hand, is tall, but wasn't in the best of shape. Those kids played hard, and I did everything I could to slow down the game so Mike could recover. When it was all said and done, Mike and I beat them two games out of three. By then, they were hungry, and they were so surprised that we'd won that they claimed we'd cheated.

In fact, we won fair and square. Still, we agreed to buy the pizza, so they followed us to the pizza place like we were pied pipers. With a captive audience, but no plan and no focus, we gave them the history of Black people from Africa to America and the greatness they descended from. We discussed with them the importance of family and community. It was too much. After two hours, which turned into four hours by the time we finally stopped talking, and a few pizzas, their eyes glazed over. We thought we had solved the world's problems, but we had done nothing but confuse them.

One kid came back to life and asked, "Hey, you guys gonna be at the basketball court next Saturday?"

I didn't even think twice. "Bet on it," I said.

We went back to that basketball court every Saturday and watched three kids turn in to twelve, then about sixty. After several weeks, word had spread about our games and our conversations. We found favor with the principal of the local middle school, Debbie Singleton, who began opening the gym for us. At the peak, there were about three hundred kids there, so we went from pizza and sodas to peanut butter and jelly and a juice box. We started off talking and asking them questions as a way to understand the teenage subculture, their codes, values, language, and all the nuances that would provide substance to this organization we were forming. The kids figured if they answered our questions and looked interested, they would be able to play some ball and have a snack. It was a win-win.

About five months passed and we used the information we gathered from the kids at the gym to strategize and create a framework, something concrete we could leverage within the community, a concept kids could connect with. I learned early on that kids need to be connected to something bigger than themselves. That's why they join gangs. They feel powerless and they're not connected to their community in any other meaningful way. Gangs are the negative side, but there are also sports, fraternities, and scouting, all of which have a set of requirements and an air of secrecy. So we created our own pseudo-secret society and found that the more mystery it had the more empowered the kids felt. Once we had a small foundation, we had to move fast.

One Saturday morning, I stood in front of about three hundred kids and broke the news to them. "I've got some good news and some bad news for you." The entire crowd was silent. "I'll start with the bad news. For some of you guys, this is the last day I'll ever see you in this gym. I know some of you are totally convinced that we have some NBA scouts hiding in the rafters and you're going to be the next Magic Johnson or Michael Jordan. I'm not saying that won't happen; it's just not gonna happen in here. So play your heart out because this is the last time I'm going to let you into the gym."

There were a few grumbles of disappointment, but they were ready to hear what I had to say next. I took a deep breath and said, "Now, let me speak to the rest of you guys because I know you've been listening and you've been suffering in silence. You want to do something meaningful with your life. You want your life to matter. You want to let the world know you were here. If that rings true to you, after this game, I want you to follow me across the street because I want to talk to you about a wonderful place Coach Anderson and I have mapped out with your well-being in mind."

I had already gotten permission from Kat to use some of our savings to rent an eight-hundred-square-foot storefront space near the gym that would serve as the very first home for Pro-Vision. After the game, I was nervous about what would happen next. We gathered the balls, turned out the lights, and locked the door. Then, Mike and I began the long walk—really only about five hundred yards across the street—to the storefront. I did not have the courage to see how many kids were behind me. I just kept walking. Then, I began mentally negotiating with God. I figured I would be satisfied if half the group followed us over. With every step I took, the number went down. As we got closer, I decided that if twenty-five kids were in, then we had succeeded. By the time I put the key in the lock and opened the door, I turned around to find more than seventy-five boys had followed us that day. I breathed a sigh of relief. That was the real start of Pro-Vision.

Young men who helped launch Pro-Vision

Mike and I collaborated, enlisted supporters, and built the foundation of what would become known as Pro-Vision. Originally, it was an afterschool academic program for enrichment, recreation, and character development of African American young men ages twelve to eighteen. We created the name of the organization through a simple, fluid process of knowing exactly what we wanted to be known for and how we wanted to impact those we serve. "Pro" is to aggressively, actively affirm that you're in favor of something. "Vision" is the insight and ability to see beyond your circumstances to what you desire. Our goal at Pro-Vision was to create and share a vision of community that everyone from the youngest to the oldest could affirm and work towards as we transcended where we were to reach where we wanted to be. From day one, Pro-Vision has been steadfast in creating that ideal.

At the beginning, in 1990, we were Pro-Vision Ministries, Inc., driven by the scripture that was the cornerstone of our service, Luke 4:18-19: "The Spirit of the Lord is on me, because he has anointed me to proclaim good news to the poor. He has sent me to proclaim freedom for the prisoners and recovery of sight for the blind, to set the oppressed free, to proclaim the year of the Lord's favor." We hosted a youth rally at Emancipation Park with games, face painting, and all kinds of activities to attract the youth and their parents. We needed that kind of event with structure, shape, and form to get us moving and to allow people to see we were serious. From that, Mike and I created a description of Pro-Vision: "A multi-faceted effort to develop and establish spiritual and moral alternatives for living. A personal approach to demonstrate God's love and purpose for life, committed to spiritual reconciliation, and to support communities caught in the vicious cycle of poverty and crime." Over the years, the words have changed slightly, but that still represents what Pro-Vision stands for.

For the first three years, I financed Pro-Vision with Kat's affirming support. Our entire staff was volunteer, so nobody received a salary, not even me. When we finally got some financial support, it came from a former teammate, Randall Cunningham. He had heard about what we were doing and was impressed. Something about the vision of the organization connected with him, and he sent Pro-Vision a substantial donation that encouraged me to believe we would make it. With that, we hired our first salaried employee, a part-time secretary who was the mom of one of the boys in our program. From there, Pro-Vision took shape. Little by little, it began to grow. Several other men eventually joined us—Gary Wallace, Kevin

Stephanie, and Ron Smith—and made up our volunteer team. More kids came to us, and we began seeing the results of the energy we were putting out. With each accomplishment and each kid we positively impacted, I felt the satisfaction and the renewed energy of showing up strong. What I was doing was for the kids, their families, and the community.

I believed then, and still believe now, that everyone can do something for someone else. The greatest investment anyone can make is to invest in the life of another human being. Even with all the educational opportunities and technical advances, it appears that human suffering has become more widespread than ever. In our effort to possess the American Dream, we have lost the importance of being our brother's keeper. We are all, as human beings, essential to our own existence. What kind of world could we build if we all showed up, if the best of us appeared every day, every time? When we show up in service to others, remarkable things can happen. The beauty comes in sustaining that. That is the foundation upon which Pro-Vision was built. I would never have guessed back then that we would still be at it nearly thirty years later. It has been a journey, one I wouldn't trade for anything.

My Love Letter to Humanity

During my days of sneaking out of the house to hang with the flambeaux carriers, to hook up with guys who would teach me to smoke, or even to attend a waistline party that ended in tragedy, I never would have guessed I would be where I am today. All the struggles I experienced trying to overcome being the underdog, to humble myself to be worthy of a life partner like Kat, or to do my best with the career and mission I was led into were worth it. All my knucklehead behaviors were necessary to bring me to myself. The blessing for me is that I was able to respond—mind, body, and soul—to the call of my purpose through my life observations.

My prodigal-son life has been a testament to what the Creator can do when you get out of your own way and let the Creator guide you to wake up and clean up. I spent most of my young life running away from the man who the Creator intended me to be. When I finally stopped running, I heard the call to stand up and show up, and I answered. Since then, my life journey has led me on a trajectory towards justice and equity. That's why everyone I serve is like me, an underdog. I get the greatest joy from seeing the least of these—those who have been marginalized, forgotten, and taken advantage of—get a seat at the table.

You don't need to have an extreme depth of personal experience or academic insight to know that when the boats of the least among us are lifted, then we all rise. Therefore, the work I do at Pro-Vision is the canary in the coal mine, a warning shot to all of us that the prosperity we seek is in jeopardy if we do not work to make it available to all who seek it. I choose to answer through my work with these kids, their families, and the community. As such, Pro-Vision is my love letter to humanity. For all my shortcomings (and there have been many), I have heeded the call and found the courage of my conviction to build something to make life better for others.

From the very start, I wanted Pro-Vision to demonstrate a model of excellence, an innovative approach to dismantle poverty and hopelessness. Mediocrity cannot be destroyed by exhibiting mediocrity. Instead, we endeavor to produce a contrast and, within the contrast, promote possibilities. Whether our supporters represent the African American elite, white allies, academics, politicians, activists, clergy, or others, when they step up to be a part of what we do, I make sure they know they're investing in their own future and essentially operating in their own best interests. For this experiment named Pro-Vision to work, we all have to show up and buy into it.

Early on, some people thought what we were doing with Pro-Vision was extraordinary, but it wasn't. We believed (and still do) that what we were doing should be the norm. In the early days, my Creator whispered to me and nudged me to do the work of uplifting a community in need. I was happy to obey. It's not extraordinary to want young people to have a strong sense of self, founded on solid character traits, or to want them to have a quality education delivered by instructors who care about their success. It's not uncommon to want everyone to have safe, affordable housing and fresh, healthy food. These things are the basics of a rewarding human existence all over the world.

The foundation of Pro-Vision is based on four key principles: character development, quality education, fresh food options, and safe, affordable housing. From 1990 to 1995, we focused squarely on education through our after school programs. We added to that in 1995, when we opened the middle school, and we've been going strong with that to this day. Working with young men is what we're best at, primarily due to our founders—Mike Anderson and me. We brought our life experiences to the table to create Pro-Vision, and we cut our teeth on those early programs, but it took us only a few years to realize what we had wouldn't be enough to make the kind of impact in the community we wanted to make. My thoughts focused on a single question: What would it take to create an ecosystem that was child-centered, adult-governed, and elderly-ruled? This thought comes from Dr. Calvin Mackie, author of *A View from the Roof- Lessons for Life and Business*. After some serious thought, and drawing upon my upbringing, I ran with it and put my own spin on it.

In 2001, the wanna-be social scientist in me created a model for a complete and thriving community, that ecosystem Dr. Mackie talked about. Around that time, Mike Anderson left Pro-Vision to pursue other areas of interest, and all these ideas began to take form in my mind. They weren't just ideas and dreams; I could see the reality of them. I just needed to take consistent, intentional action in the right direction. I knew that in order for people to get to a healthy place, they had to have healthy options and healthy habits.

All this took me back to that spark of justice and equity that was ignited in me as a kid who was rejected from the football team and shunned by teachers, the kid who knew there was more inside me than what others saw, but who didn't know how to push it out. I was the underdog, and I get the greatest joy when I witness the least among us get their fair share in life. That is what pushed me forward with Pro-Vision and it's what keeps me moving towards the vision, despite the many roadblocks we have faced over the years.

Education: The Passport to the Future

The devastation I felt back in elementary school after overhearing those teachers talk about me stayed with me throughout the rest of my academic experience. It was part of the reason I did just enough to get by in high school, and it was partly why I entered college unprepared and insecure about my ability to perform academically. Learning is something we all do intrinsically; we simply cannot help it. However, the way we learn is specific to each person. Unfortunately, the traditional American education system is not set up to identify the individual student's learning style and deliver relevant information to support that student's needs, gifts, and abilities. This was the driver for developing the afterschool program and later the middle school program at Pro-Vision.

To put it lightly, I am at war with the education system as we know it because it shortchanges our kids, but also blindfolds and handcuffs our parents and our communities, the vital support systems needed to ensure well-rounded kids. Standard education says, "Give us your child, get out of the way, and let us brainwash them." The necessary partnerships with parents and communities are missing when, really, they go hand in glove. Not only that, but the traditional approach to education is egregious and it's offensive, particularly to African American and Indigenous people, in its obvious attempts to erase the truth of our history and contributions to this country. In fact, whenever our government runs into a fiscal deficit, one of the first areas slashed is education, and then we bemoan the fact that we don't have an educated workforce. In a capitalistic society, everything becomes a commodity. And as a commodity, the education of our children gets manipulated.

Education in the Western Hemisphere needs an overhaul. At Pro-Vision, we have put forward a model that includes not only a safe learning environment for kids, but also an environment that treats each student as an individual with specific gifts and talents. We also make it a requirement for parents to be involved. That means they must volunteer at our school, no exceptions. When we give more than just lip service to the adage that it takes a village to raise a child, we see parents, families, and communities stand up and show up to support kids. The function of education is to spark the imagination of young minds. We make education fun, so students are not bored. We've developed a model that sees our kids as individuals and presents information in a way that is engaging and interactive. Because of that, our kids cannot wait to get to school.

The education of young people is a multi-layered issue. For some, it focuses on job readiness, and for others, the goal is completion of course requirements. In reality, education is a lifelong process that takes young people from the very basics of who they are naturally and leads them through a lifelong journey to discover, appreciate, and hone their God-given gifts and talents for the betterment of society. Formal education has a function, but lived experience and positive inputs from trusted, well-meaning influences also impact that lifelong learning journey. The result of this should be well-informed individuals who, each day, practice wisdom in everything they do.

We have become sidetracked in thinking everyone needs to go to college and those who do not are at a disadvantage. Everyone needs a twenty-first century education, but that does not always lead to college. There is dignity in coming home with grease under your fingernails or sawdust on your shoes. My Uncle Nick was a perfect example of that. He could use his hands *and* his mind. He made a business out of doing what he did best, carpentry, and he never stopped learning and filling his mind with positive information and insights that broadened his worldview.

What we do at Pro-Vision is a spin on how some Scandinavian countries, like Sweden, identify a child's gifts and talents. We have a long way to go on that front, but their concept is aspirational for us. By the sixth grade, kids know what areas they are gifted in, and from that point, their education is geared specifically towards those talents. Then, by eighth grade, young people go on to formal education or internships specific to their field of interest and their unique ability. That could be anything from carpentry to banking to medicine.

In America, we don't do that. We have done a disservice to kids with the cookie-cutter, one-dimensional approach that suggests everybody should have a liberal arts education. We assume a flat, linear IQ test can fully test your gifts, strengths, and abilities, but that is not true. In his book *Multiple Intelligences in the Classroom*, Dr. Thomas Armstrong suggests everyone has multiple intellects that include anything from physical to verbal to spatial and others. Standard IQ tests don't identify all these traits. Traditional education is not designed to nurture a child's natural gifts, so those gifts go largely ignored unless a student is identified as gifted and allowed into a special program.

We put forth a different model at Pro-Vision. It's not perfect or complete, but it makes education fun and interesting for kids. We take the kids who are viewed by some as the least valuable to society—those who have been given up on—and we remediate their experience. Often, they go from being at the bottom of the class to being on the honor roll. I know what that is like because I've been there; I was that kid all those years ago. Kids can master the basics of learning—reading, writing, and arithmetic—but we help them build their confidence, their character, and their commitment, not just to pass a test, but to succeed in life. It just takes a different approach. I took the same principles I learned on the playing field and structured them to apply academically. Proper inputs plus consistent effort builds mastery.

> *Education is the passport to the future and a valuable part of renewing a community.*
> *~Coach Roynell Young*

Every kid has the potential to master something in life. We help our kids get there because we expect them to be great. The danger of having low expectations of our kids is that it kills their efforts and therefore threatens the success of their future. Our expectations go beyond helping students absorb the basics of a quality education. We have a structured institution to help feed their intellect, instill positive character traits, and teach socialization. These are important characteristics of an engaged citizenry that understands voting and politics, finances, and other areas. With these foundations, kids become well-rounded, responsible, complete adults who act in their own self-interest and in the interest of their family and community. We influence young people to make wise decisions about their lives so their choices are more deliberate and their outcomes more favorable. That is what's needed for our kids to survive and thrive in this world.

Each of us came here in a metaphysical way on a mission to impact this world at this time, to make it better than we found it, to change lives, and to be the best expression of ourselves we can be. None of us came here empty-handed. The Creator provided everything we need to survive and succeed. We need only tap into it, but most of us need guidance and support to uncover the natural gifts we came here with.

The goal is to study young people to figure out their gift. I love doing this with the kids at Pro-Vision because it fans the flame of encouragement and builds success. I intentionally seek the carrots that pull them forward to help them understand their gifts. In this way, they are motivated to follow through on a commitment, rather than doing something out of obligation.

Family traditions and influences can be strong motivators of behavior, good or bad. There was a kid in my program who came from a family of criminally minded men. The kid had promise, but despite all my efforts to guide him and save him from himself, I lost him to the streets. He had a God-given gift for detail. Some think that's no big deal, but being able to see the small things amid the big picture is not something everyone can do well. This kid had such attention to detail he could pick out things from a mile away and say, "Hey, Coach, you know what, this needs to be moved over there." No one else would have ever noticed it, but he was always right. I was amazed at that. I often thought about what that gift could be translated into. Could he have become an accountant, an engineer, a surgeon? Maybe he could have found his life's passion in the culinary arts or construction, teaching or landscaping. There are a million things he could have done with his God-given gift, but I lost him.

The people who were sponsoring him asked me to work with him. They meant well, but they didn't have a clue as to how to help him in the way that would benefit him best. They were operating from the spiritual point of view of Jesus washing the feet of the disciples. They wanted him to humble himself in some biblical way and devote his life to serving others without first knowing himself. That's fine and good, but they didn't know they were dealing with a roughneck. I knew because I had been a roughneck too when I was his age and in his state. I needed something to shock me back into reality, and I figured that was what this kid needed too.

I took this young man on a Pro-Vision retreat, with about fifteen other boys, at a board member's ranch. We cleared trees during the daytime, and our recreation time was spent doing things kids in the country do—fishing, riding four-wheelers, racing, tossing horseshoes. At night, I had the most intense sessions with these young men about the very subject of discovering their natural gifts. On the third night, I cracked this young man into a million pieces. He started crying and he could not close the floodgates. He cried like he was two years old, purging himself of all kinds of things. By the time the weekend was over, I was sure I had reached him. I knew he was changed, and I felt good about that.

When we got back to town, he went back into his old environment, not as a changed man but as his old self. Everything I had started at the ranch was sucked out of him in less than twenty-four hours. His well-meaning sponsors believed all they needed to do was hug him through his pain. Sadly, within about two months, he ended up arrested and placed before a judge. His sponsors asked me to intervene on his behalf. I'm not sure what they expected me to do for this kid, but I accepted the invitation to step in, knowing I had to handle this my way. As I stood before the court, I noticed this young man sitting there, head down, looking ashamed to be back in this place where he had been before. He and I were the only two in that courtroom who knew what had happened months earlier at the ranch. He couldn't look me in the eye, but I knew the regret and the shame in his heart.

When the judge called me forward and offered me the chance to speak on behalf of the young man, I said, "Your Honor, I think you should give this young man a second chance." He raised his eyebrows, not in surprise, but with curiosity. I continued, "But we have to put something in place to hold him accountable, or else he's going to run out of control." The low rumble of discomfort and surprise spread throughout the courtroom like I had just accused the boy of murder. "I will only agree to work with him if his guardians agree to parenting classes and volunteer opportunities at the school, and if this young man agrees to be checked, on a regular basis, for substances," I said. His sponsors, in particular, were notably upset with me. However, none of what I suggested was punitive. It was designed to save him from himself.

His pastor, who happened to be a white guy, challenged what I was saying. He said it was too harsh. Instead, he wanted to take this kid to a camp where they modeled the Jesus way, washing feet like the disciples did. That was not the way to get this kid to wake up. He was asleep to his purpose and he didn't know his gifts. He was living in darkness and headed for destruction. Having lived that kind of life myself, I knew that without serious intervention that kid would become another statistic.

In the same way that my younger self needed someone like Coach Casem to arrest my thinking and interrupt my way of being, that kid needed the approach I had suggested. When he came to Pro-Vision Academy, I became the Coach Casem for him, and that, by default, came with struggle. Unfortunately, his well-meaning supporters thought he could regain his life without the gift of struggle. That was unrealistic. His pathology was systemic and generational, and he had become preoccupied with what was taking place in the underworld. Unfortunately, his dark side, and everything included with it, overtook him. That experience taught me the truth of the adage "You win some, you lose some." Losing, in cases like this, is never easy.

I have never put myself out there as an educator because I'm not. I simply have a deep, abiding love for the people I serve. What I am doing with Pro-Vision through our four-legged approach is to unpack poverty and raise our country's expectations of what education can do for children. Unfortunately, as it stands, the American education system cannot get out of its own way because it's all about business and profit. This country gives a lot of lip service to the importance of education, yet our global grade with regard to graduation rates and outcomes is consistently down with those of third-world countries. That has to change.

My ultimate goal is for Pro-Vision to no longer rely on state or federal funding so we can realize the educational, cultural, and moral framework I envision. For that to happen, we would have to move towards being private. That's when the real work of supporting young people's intellectual development will begin and when we will see the kind of results we already see, only on a larger scale.

A Strong Character Builds a Strong Foundation

When my grandmother smacked me upside the head the day I almost got arrested for selling fireworks, I had no idea what she was communicating to me. I just felt embarrassed. Her back-handed slap was a message telling me she expected more from me, that I had been raised better than that. My immature mind had created a weird sense of self that equated going to juvy with being seen as a tough guy. At that point in my life, I had not developed a well-rounded character—a positive self-esteem where I was confident in my abilities, a respect for myself and for others, the capacity to set positive goals for my future, the ability to critically assess every situation, and the courage to stand up for what is fair and just. It took me many years to develop these characteristics. The influences of adults like my grandmother, my parents, Uncle Nick, and even Smooth—the guy who pleaded with the cops not to take me to juvy—were in no small part instrumental to my character development. If I needed that kind of influence back then, kids today need it in exponential degrees.

The supersonic, multimedia, digital age we live in fires information at us at such an alarming rate that we do not have time to process it. The dissemination of information has shifted from reading to consuming social media, television, podcasts, text messages, video games, and more, all spewing thousands of messages into our brains so quickly that we are almost in suspended animation, unable to properly process our own thoughts. The net of protection is down, and kids find themselves exposed to more information than ever, much of which is incorrect or watered down for the benefit of those who distribute the information. Consequently, young people do not know what to think about anything at any given moment, so rather than think, they react, and that is dangerous. This is true for adults, and it is especially true for young people.

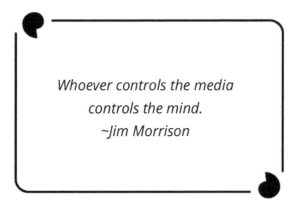

Whoever controls the media controls the mind.
~Jim Morrison

Getting young men and young women to see the world through fresh eyes is essential for developing critical thinkers, thoughtful young people who rely on a moral compass to help them make healthy decisions. External variables can be damaging and can cut off thoughtful introspection and the natural curiosity young people have about the world. When they are fed false information and disjointed or incorrect facts, they are confused and tend to reject the generational continuum, choosing instead to create their own set of morals and beliefs that drive their behavior. Many of the institutions that traditionally fostered high morals and behavior in the African American community have become weak, impotent, or disbanded, thereby leaving families—the cornerstone of a healthy, thriving community—waning. As a result, the positive influences that informed and nurtured kids—parents, elders, and extended family, as well as teachers, clergy, and authority figures—have taken a back seat to the opinions of their peers.

In the Pro-Vision ecosystem, we proactively and positively mold young people's character, guiding them to become lifelong learners fully engaged in their community and equipped for life. That includes exposure to and knowledge about politics, culture, and history, as well as critical thinking. With a structured program to teach character development, we give kids a moral compass and teach them to be positive leaders in their own community. In this way, we are redeeming people who have been marginalized and thrown away. We are giving them power over their minds, their lives, and their communities. To do that effectively, we require the parents to fully participate in the child's development.

In order for us to enter into an equal relationship with families, we have to be forthright about what's expected of them at the beginning. Each parent meets with our administration office to discuss what is expected of their child and of them, as the parent. We know character development for kids doesn't work when parents simply drop off their kids at school and expect us to make it happen, and then only show up when there's a problem. We enter into a partnership in which we not only discuss what is needed for the child's educational and character development, but we also discuss the parent's needs and challenges to determine if we can offer services to support them, whether that's job training, food support, or mental health resources to help make that parent complete. As the child grows and develops, the parent does as well. In this way, we move families away from the state of learned helplessness so we can build strong character development within young people.

> *Be careful of the habits you*
> *introduce into your life*
> *because it might take a*
> *lifetime to chase them out.*
> *~Coach Roynell Young*

Many of the kids in our program come to us with their foundation crumbled. Their home lives are unstable, their self-esteem is damaged, and even their physical fitness has been ignored. They need a jumping-off point, a springboard that helps launch them to become better versions of themselves. To grab their attention right away, I have to let them know that, as long as they are in this world, in an imperfect body, they will struggle in one way or another. However, struggle does not have to destroy them; it can set them up to conquer the world. Before they can conquer the world, they have to first conquer themselves, and that is why we focus on building their character. In doing that, they take the first step to realizing why they were put here and what they should be doing with their life.

We are here to offer empathy, not sympathy, so we can help them get up and walk again, to wake up, stand up, and show up in this world. Whether you grew up with a father or not, whether you had certain material things or not, the world does not care. No one is going to give you a pass because of a hard-luck story. We know that hugging the kids' problems out of them will not fix them. Pro-Vision is not a crutch for these kids or their families; it is a means to help them realize their own power and what they are capable of accomplishing. We do not teach helplessness; we teach self-efficacy and self-discipline and how those two characteristics can impact every aspect of their lives.

In the early 1990s, the plight of the African American male was dismal. Gangster rap, gang life, and the crack epidemic were strong influences on young men in marginalized communities. Families were destabilized, the education system was ignoring Black kids, and the criminal justice system was creating more ways to trap them into a never-ending cycle of despair. Many of the institutions that had previously sheltered and supported families had become weakened, including the Black church. The family unit was waning, causing a dynamic shift in the nuclear family. The people and support systems that had informed and nurtured kids had become impotent. That is the vacuum Pro-Vision stepped into.

In response, we created the Manhood Program, a continuous, year-round program that creates a brotherhood, a fraternity, in which young men are exposed to concrete information about politics, culture, history, and exhibiting appropriate behavior in different situations. All of this integrates to help develop their character as indigenous leaders and positive contributors to their community, but to create an effective program that impacted young men in a positive way, we first had to understand what teenage subculture looks like. What were the norms? What was the entry fee to run with the herd? Once we realized that, we created our own world for them.

As Mike and I connected with other youth-focused organizations and probed the streets of Sunnyside, recruiting kids into our program early on, we came upon a gang leader, a tough guy who knew the streets well. He told me, "Look, man, I appreciate what you're doing, but you guys are never going to out-recruit us." He was so confident in what he said that he captivated my attention. "We know that kids look for belonging," he said. "They want to be connected to other people and something bigger than themselves." That was the simple secret we had to exploit if we were going to succeed. That guy taught me about how kids want to be acknowledged, how they are looking for power and accountability, and how they will hold on to any semblance of that *esprit de corps*.

From that unlikely conversation, we created the Manhood Program, a four-step developmental, risk-reward program that morphed into a pseudo-secret society (or so we had the young men believing it was), complete with a secret handshake and a code that nobody except those in our Pro-Vision group knew about. That structure makes these kids feel special and separate. Along each level, they have to master specific, intentional information in politics, economics, race relations, service, and other areas, all intended to build a foundation for a successful life. They learn about the intricacies of the complicated world in which they live and how to make smart choices based on their own values, rather than allowing their choices to be manipulated by external forces.

Through the Manhood Program, we endeavor to produce lifelong learners who are fully engaged in their community. From the onset, our objective was to guide these young men to understand three critical things inside of the Pro-Vision ethos. First, as they grow into manhood, they must demonstrate the ability to legally provide for themselves. In the socio-economic system we live in, no one is going to do for you what you are not willing to do for yourself. Second, if they are fortunate to find a partner, they must be able to provide for their family. Last, they must be willing to serve the community they live in.

Every life was created for a reason. Through my own practices, behaviors, and interests, I have figured out my reason for being, and I share that knowledge with the young men in our Manhood Program to help them awaken to their reason for being created. In a sense, we are redeeming people who have been marginalized and forgotten. It's amazing to see these young men begin to view the world as thoughtful, critical thinkers, who not only rely on their intellect, but also develop a moral compass to help them make decisions and earn the respect of others.

One of the privileges of participation in the Manhood Program is the chance to earn a coveted paid internship at a local business, corporation, university, or organization. These kids are working all kinds of jobs, from blue collar to white collar, from assisting scientists at a brain cancer research center to managing the distribution channel in a warehouse or learning agricultural science on a farm. This kind of responsibility teaches young people to be independent and responsible, and it sets our kids up for career success, as well as positioning them as role models for younger kids.

As the program for boys grew in popularity, we realized we needed to do the same outreach to the young ladies in our community. The foundation of Pro-Vision was to support Black boys, but we know a community isn't complete without strong, stable, confident, and intelligent young women who respect themselves and have the chance to wake up, clean up, stand up, and show up successfully as positive contributors to society. Our S.H.E. Program fills that requirement. Representing the ideal of Strong, Healthy, Enlightened young ladies, S.H.E. mirrors the Manhood Program with opportunities to participate in the internship program, as well as educational and character development programs designed specifically for girls. The breadth of Pro-Vision's programming has become more inclusive because we know that human beings have more in common than we have differences. Before we are black or white, male or female, we are human beings created by God, so we do not let the human constructs get in the way of the clarity we deliver.

We instill in our kids the concept of clean-up, which focuses on personal responsibility and self-reliance, the reality that you should not expect anyone to do for you what you are not willing to do for yourself. We tell the kids, "If you don't want to participate in your own liberation, step aside because nobody is going to do it for you. Entitlement is a no-no." This disease of entitlement runs rampant, not only among privileged kids, but also for the kids I serve at Pro-Vision. Their entitlement says, "Hey, I was born in these circumstances. Give me a break. The world owes me something." My thought is if you want to be a part of what we have, doing anything less than your best is unacceptable, and if you won't give your best, you should find another organization to be part of.

If you are willing to rise to the Pro-Vision way, I will hear your concerns, and I will give you the tools to overcome them, but you have to put them to work for yourself. You have to figure out what you are willing to invest to build a bridge from your past to your future. Sometimes, that bridge needs to be built away from familiar surroundings to put kids in a state of uncertainty, where they are unfamiliar with the environment and can test their drive and commitment. We developed an entry point for that through our mission/self-discovery trips.

Just like my experience as a kid, a lot of these young people have never been outside of the confines of the community they grew up in. That reality is part and parcel of their limited worldview. We expand their perspective while also providing an intimate, safe environment for engagement, physical fitness, community service activities, and extended character development exercises. That effort has become our annual mission trip and has taken kids to Louisiana, Mississippi, parts of Texas, and even to Maine and Pennsylvania. With only about forty available spots, the mission trips are a highlight of the year, and the participation has to be earned, so those spots are coveted.

Each mission trip is built around a controlled, structured environment that includes a community service project that the kids do—building a playground, tearing down an old house and reusing the lumber, working at a thrift shop, painting classrooms at a school—to help instill teamwork and cooperation. At the end of the day, they have some recreation time to blow off steam and to help lower their inhibitions for the nightly transparency sessions. That's when we want the teens to be relaxed and open so we can encourage them to confront some of the skeletons in their closet, basically to unpack their mental and emotional baggage. It is therapeutic with a moral undertone. Every night builds upon the previous nights, allowing kids to be transparent, raw, and open. They have a chance to begin the journey to clean up their lives, to dig deep and expose what's happening on the inside—the thoughts, emotions, fears, and hopes that drive them every day—and to make the commitment to move forward, intentionally, in a positive way.

Some of the kids make decisions on these trips that alter their lives forever. Even after they have been through the program and have entered adulthood, some of them can still recite the codes and the motto. They are mere words, a simple set of rules and behaviors for them to follow that we shaped into a secret society. We added meaning to it, and it has become their reality, the tools that ultimately shape their lives, whether they are conscious of it or not. The atmosphere of trust and respect that we create within the Manhood and S.H.E. Programs makes the code so real that many of the young people have called upon it at different times in their lives.

Unfortunately, there are also kids who go right back to square one as soon as they return to their parents and their familiar environment. Having a kid on the right track one day and then off track the next is not the best-case scenario to effect the change they need. The work we do with them puts them on a trajectory to become more advanced in their thinking, but they need to be immersed in the right environment for continuous advancement, mentally and behaviorally, so we also focus heavily on our parental approach to supporting kids.

As we work with parents and guardians, they learn how to influence their children and instill a value system in them. With many of the parents being raised in the Me Generation, even those who have few resources have suffered the burden of wanting to give their kids everything. That has served neither the kids nor the rest of society. In fact, it has produced a new generation of young people saddled with entitlement. Pro-Vision flips that thinking and lifts up personal responsibility, self-reliance, and honest work as entry points to achieve goals. As a result of going through our programs, the kids are being empowered; they just don't know it. In addition, they are building their own story of success that they can carry with them throughout their lives.

Healthy Eating, Healthy Living

When I was a kid, my grandmother would prepare oatmeal, eggs, toast, and orange juice for all six of us. It was a nutritious, stick-to-your-ribs kind of meal. When we started the Pro-Vision Academy in 1995, I was shocked to my core at what the kids brought to school as their breakfast. One morning, I saw a kid walking to class with a sixteen-ounce orange soda and a block of chocolate.

I stopped him as he hurried to class, his backpack hanging off his shoulder. "Young man, what is this?" I asked.

"It's my breakfast, Coach!"

At that moment, it occurred to me that we had a great deal to unpack in our community. We live in an era of parents who do not cook. There are few grandmothers like mine who spend their mornings preparing nutritious breakfasts for their grandchildren, and that doesn't take into account the other meals of the day. How many families sit down to a homecooked meal together these days? In all fairness, many parents and guardians I have encountered do not have the luxury of what I grew up under. With all the demands of trying to protect and provide for a family—especially for those who are single parents—the task of preparing even a single meal to be enjoyed with the entire family can be almost insurmountable. That is why creating an external, village-like experience is important to building family relationships. Dinner enjoyed with the entire family is more than just a meal. The interaction around that meal really matters. This is what builds strong family bonds, open communication, healthy bodies, and sharp minds. At the same time, the foods families consume are just as important as sharing a meal together.

Growing up in New Orleans, we welcomed family meals and community gatherings where food was the focal point. Unfortunately, the nutritional value of some foods has become lost in the varieties of flavors we have introduced into the complex dishes we prepare. In my hometown specifically, and in the South in general, we have developed sophisticated tastebuds and an affinity for dishes like seafood gumbo, deep fried chicken, or étouffées, not to mention the other Cajun and Creole dishes. In the process, we forget that not everything that tastes good is good for you.

This phenomenon of nutritional indifference is not only a Southern thing. When I first went to Philadelphia, I was eating heavy foods and a lot of meat. Basically, I became a true meat-and-potatoes kind of guy. That stuff was good for keeping me solid for football, but as the years went by, my body needed a reset. After I left the NFL and moved to Houston full time, Kathleen prepared all our food and made sure our meals were more nutritious, more colorful, and less laden with the sauces, gravies, and heavy side dishes I was used to eating as a kid. Being removed from that New Orleans food culture, and from the eating habits I had adopted as a pro athlete, caused me to rethink my diet and eat healthier all around. Kat protected our family, took the time to choose nutritious food options, and made every meal tasty. In the Black community, we have to return to the way our ancestors viewed food, not simply as consumption, but as medicine.

The Pro-Vision McNair Urban Farm was created as a way to start the conversation about healthy eating, healthy living, and the history and bonding our communities have around good food. The farm is designed to speak loudly to the food deserts that exist in practically every low-income community in America. It's an open laboratory where food is grown and distributed to local restaurants, which generates residual income for Pro-Vision. It is designed to have both a community influence and a commercial impact. In fact, the farm stands as a symbol of self-reliance and industriousness that visitors to our facility do not expect to experience. It demonstrates to the outside world that we are serious thinkers committed to addressing the nutrition disparities in our community, which is why we offer tours of the Urban Farm.

A few years ago, while I was leading a tour, a white gentleman asked me time and again, "Who came up with this concept?" Each time, I told him it was our idea to create the farm and it is our sweat equity that keeps it producing fresh, organic, nutritious food. He couldn't seem to believe Black folks had it in them to do something like that. Food cultivation is a cornerstone of the history of African Americans and is part and parcel of our DNA. Unfortunately, that DNA is tainted with some poor eating habits that have been forced upon us for generations.

The foods enslaved people were forced to eat on plantations were just short of garbage. I learned about some of these foods while reading a cookbook of slave recipes, and I realized that they had to make something out of nothing because all the food they had was scrap food, throwaways from the enslaver's kitchen. In many instances, it was the worst of the worst and they were forced to eat it, yet they managed to survive on it. The centuries and generations of that kind of cooking and eating has altered the DNA of Black people in America and probably created some of the health disparities we see today.

My sole question after reading that book was: Why are we still eating this way today? The simple answer is that it's tradition, but when tradition does not line up with logic and reason, tradition has to be abandoned because it could be sending us to an early grave. When you don't have much, you make do with what you have, but when you know better, you do better. In our modern, fast-food society, many Black people and other marginalized communities still don't have easy access to fresh, healthy foods. In the neighborhood surrounding Pro-Vision, popular options like Popeye's Chicken and Domino's Pizza are the easy, cheap choices for kids to fill their hungry bellies. We want better for the kids and families in our communities, and the Pro-Vision McNair Urban Farm helps fill the nutritional gap.

The Urban Farm started in 2008 as a therapeutic arm of Pro-Vision. We created a small raised-bed garden on a back lot of the property that we used as part of the earth science instruction. There wasn't much to it at the time, so whenever kids misbehaved in class, they would be sent to the garden as a form of discipline, a chance to work through their issues and decompress while spending time outside. The next thing we knew, kids were requesting to work in the garden. That was not the intended effect, but it was better than we planned because it helped kids destress and gain a knowledge of how food grows and how it evolves from a seed to something edible on your plate. From that experience, they learned to appreciate the skill and patience of gardening and how to incorporate fresh foods into their lifestyle.

Later that year, we experienced a drought, and the ground was so dry it cracked open and caked over the entire garden. I am grateful to Local Foods restaurants in Houston for supporting us during that time. Mother Nature was doing a job on our produce and it wasn't much to brag about, but they believed in what we were doing and continued to buy lettuce and other crops from us. Around that time, Greg Hambrick, who had a heart for a unique farming concept, wanted to partner with someone in the urban corridor to create aquaponic greenhouses. He wanted space to construct six, 50-foot x 100-foot, state-of-the-art greenhouses. We had the space and the need, so I immediately welcomed his project. It has since flourished to produce healthy crops of lettuce, kale, and mustard greens in the green houses, as well as peppers, eggplant, beets, olives, zucchini, squash, and cantaloupe in the traditional raised beds.

The Urban Farm is evolving into a program that benefits Pro-Vision, the surrounding community, our kids and their families, and the local restaurant industry in Houston. One aspect of the farm is to build community engagement by serving as a community garden to encourage healthy eating, to educate families about various crops they can grow, and to demonstrate how to prepare those vegetables. On Saturdays, we hold workshops where cooks come in, take vegetables directly from the garden, and show young parents and kids how to prepare them. In this way, they are introduced to different types of vegetables and how they're grown. They learn how to cook those foods, and they know what fresh, nutritious food tastes like. We envision a farmers market as a natural outgrowth of the community garden, where families who secure their plot of land also care for it and sell the produce to families in the community.

Always with a focus of self-reliance and self-sustainability, Pro-Vision generates revenue from the Urban Farm by distributing the fresh, organic produce grown on the farm to local restaurants. Our contribution to the burgeoning farm-to-table movement is a source of pride for our kids and for our community. Because giving back is part of the fabric of Pro-Vision, we also look for ways to support our community with the product of our efforts. When the COVID-19 pandemic exacerbated the reality of food insecurity in our community, Pro-Vision partnered with another local nonprofit to distribute fresh produce to over one thousand families a week for four months. We walk the talk and our give-back is not only real; it's also heartfelt.

People in marginalized communities have to learn how to control what we can control because external forces are not kind to us. We have to be intentional about the areas of our lives where our direct input effects the best output for us. Being proactive about and protective of what goes into our minds and our bodies is the best defense against a societal structure set up to keep marginalized people on the fringes, always wanting, always wishing, always waiting. I am proud that Pro-Vision takes an active stance to build up our young people and our communities in areas that are sustainable and lead to a positive future.

Safe at Home

The things that happened in the Magnolia Projects were part of everyday life for the people who lived there. Although the majority of those people were hard-working, decent individuals, there were also robberies and wild parties, fights and ladies of the night, and a lot of activity within that low-income housing development. Even though it was only blocks from my own neighborhood in uptown New Orleans, it was a world away in terms of the energy that seemed to hypnotize people into doing things I'm sure they knew were detrimental to their community. As a kid, I was careful not to become a victim of the crime-ridden area on my way to and from Thomy Lafon School. Later, I was drawn to the projects out of curiosity, which is how I ended up at that party the night Greg McGee was killed.

Although I experienced some trauma related to that area, not all my experiences there were doom and gloom. In fact, I have many fond memories of The Magnolia, from the iconic talent shows and skate mobile races to the track meets and my failed effort to make it onto the Shakespeare Park football team. All in all, my experience with the Magnolia Projects and the residents who lived there informed me about what living in poverty looks like, the damage it can inflict on young people and families, and how the rest of society views neighborhoods where Black people have little voice about their surroundings and few options to pursue a better life. All of it was part of the insight and impetus for developing Pro-Vision's housing program.

Everyone deserves to live in a safe, secure, clean community. We offer that to Houston's residents as our way of bringing to life Dr. Martin Luther King's dream of the beloved community— child-centered, adult governed, and elderly ruled—a nearly deferred dream of the promise America offered all its citizens. In essence, Pro-Vision is making good on the American Dream for those whose ancestors toiled the land to make America what it is. We are making real what the Constitution and the American philosophy promise.

Our master-planned development is the result of a selfless $5 million donation from the McNair Foundation that helped us acquire sixty acres as a canvas to construct a monumental vision. This community concept includes a 350-unit, mixed-income, gated community, a three-story senior apartment complex with commercial units on the first floor, plus 130 townhouses, another one hundred homes for experienced homeowners, and miles of nature trails all in the heart of Houston's Sunnyside community. With the Pro-Vision Academy nearby to deliver educational and afterschool programs to kids, plus the Urban Farm to provide nutritious, organic foods, Pro-Vision is demonstrating that a dream once held as aspirational is now within reach.

This is a place where families can live, work, learn, play, and engage in a safe environment. It incites a pride of ownership that every human longs for, but which many are denied in today's economy. When people see themselves as a stakeholder in something bigger than themselves, rather than as a burden on society, they rise up with pride and take stewardship over their surroundings. I know our people have the desire and the capacity to live this way, and Pro-Vision has the foresight to make it happen.

When I invited those guys living on the streets of Philadelphia to my apartment to clean up, I had no idea that was a foreshadowing of what I'm doing with the Pro-Vision housing program. Our society ignores those who live in less-desirable situations, telling the lie that people want to live in squalor or unsafe environments. The truth of our human nature is that we all want comfort and safety. Settling for anything less is an indication of unaddressed issues that the individual needs to wake up to so they can clean up, stand up, and do better for themselves. Some people need a little help to do that. Pro-Vision addresses as many of those issues as we can to help people get back to their true nature, their true desires, and move forward with living out their true purpose. Everyone deserves that opportunity, but not everyone has access in this America.

At Pro-Vision, we are dealing with people's lives. They have been disappointed, disconnected, and disenfranchised. They have promise and a desire to be more, but the card deck of life has been stacked in such a way that they keep getting a bum hand. We exist to lead as the ace in the hole, the secret weapon to lend a hand, and to be a guide to overcome life's challenges. Poverty brings with it a whole host of heavy baggage, and the only way we can unpack poverty is to have a model of excellence. Through a cultural and moral approach to living, we demonstrate to families pride of ownership and having power over your mind, your body, and your environment. We show young kids the best of being black and brown, so they see what excellence looks like and they know it is possible and expected of them.

Over the last few decades, this country has witnessed a rapid erosion of concern for our fellow human beings, driven by greed, profits, and racial and cultural indifference. COVID-19 quickly and painfully brought existing disparities to the surface and cut across socio-economic privilege in a way that caused a dramatic chasm in the obvious social divide, leaving lasting and harmful results that have shaken us to our foundation. It was a wake-up call. The lack of concern for the least of our citizens by those who have the most can no longer be manipulated or spun as just the way things are supposed to be. The human construct is now exposed, and some truths have been revealed—one of which is that the American ideal this country holds so dear has been intentionally and systematically withheld from Black people. It is disingenuous and downright disrespectful for people to suddenly and half-heartedly acknowledge the disparities that have existed since our ancestors hit these shores.

This tragic revelation has forced people to see the truth about how our nation treats those less fortunate and how our leaders' poor planning and inaction in the recent past has led us to a place of near desperation. The disparities in housing, food, education, health care, and employment are in place because those in power have failed to see every American as valuable. It

224

has been that way from the founding of this country, when the masses of the "have-not" population—poor whites, immigrants, and Black people who built this country—were manipulated and pitted against each other. In the midst of spewing the lie to the world that America is a global democratic ideal, our wounds were exposed, our values laid bare for all to see, and the dismal, deplorable way we treat the least of these was revealed. As Malcolm X foretold, "The chickens are coming home to roost."

Either in response to, in defense against, or in opposition to (I'm still not sure which) the realities of racial and economic disparities revealed in 2020, my bold vision for this community is that it will become a drop that ripples out across the nation to be replicated in communities that have long called out for the chance to clean up and show up. In a sense, I feel like a drum major leading the way for a new America where the masses unite to turn the old approach upside down. It is well past time for us all to experience the norm of thriving, galvanized communities where residents are responsible stakeholders who understand the power of engaging with one another and who seek opportunities to stand up and show up as Americans and global citizens.

A JOURNEY
WORTH TAKING

In his song "The Other Side," Gil Scott Heron talks about how low he was when he was hooked on drugs. He emerged from the darkness because he heard the voices of the ancestors calling him to a higher place, a place of freedom. Every time I hear that song, something speaks to me and I get chills. I've been in that darkness, and I too have heard the voices of the ancestors calling me into the light, urging me to wake up, guiding me to clean up, helping me to stand up, and inviting me to show up. I have listened. I have arrived. I'm far from perfect, but I feel satisfied with the life I now live. It brings me joy to show up and give people what they need. I'm able to do that because I have a little bit of clarity now. That clarity has come from my lived experiences, the contrast I've seen going from darkness to light, the footsteps I have walked in that have guided me back home.

Throughout my life, I've had to arrest my thinking, to narrow my focus, and to settle my mind to eliminate the multitude of distractions that threatened to keep me from fulfilling my purpose. Those distractions have come in many forms and at every turn along my life journey, from childhood illness to witnessing violence in my youth, falling into the trap of drugs as a teen, and assaults on my confidence as an adult. The counter to all that was the good that life always held in reserve for me—a family who loved me and tried to protect me, a woman who saw me as a diamond in the rough, a career that provided financial stability, and a community that welcomed my incomplete vision of help and hope.

Now, I am at the point of living the reality of what I hoped life would be when I was that eleven-year-old kid in New Orleans, selling firecrackers on the street corner. I now show up anchored in something bigger than myself, living the continuation of what my ancestors hoped was possible. I am living my dream, a life of servant leadership and self-efficacy. A life that pays homage to the struggles of the past and builds a foundation for the continuum of healing and self-reliance not only for Black people, but also for all individuals who find themselves disenfranchised. This is my hope.

> *History is a clock that people use to tell their political and cultural time of day. It is a compass they use to find themselves on the map of human geography. It tells them where they are but, more importantly, what they must be.*
> *~John Henrik Clark*

I have always been fascinated by history because it transports the inquisitive and curious nature of my personality. In many ways, it has served as a refuge, a place of shelter when life becomes confusing. It provides clarity for me. Just like an old and faithful friend, it is the place I can always retreat to, to find solace, peace, and affirmation. When I read about courageous, selfless figures like David Walker, who launched a righteous appeal to dismantle the barbaric system of slavery, I am inspired to continue my work. This was during one of history's most violent and dangerous times for Black people. For him to have found the inner fortitude to take on such a risky endeavor makes me wonder if I could rise up to my own crucible moments. There are constant and numerous obstacles that challenge me in my daily walk, as I seek to transcend and live out my purpose. Each day I take on challenges, inspired by those who have come before me.

Two of my heroes, Senator Charles Sumner and Congressman Thaddeus Stevens, were unapologetic patriots. These two lawmakers were tireless in their efforts to get this country to live up to its ideals of liberty, justice, and equity for all. In fact, Senator Sumner was almost beaten to death by another senator from South Carolina because of Sumner's long-held belief in equity and justice for all. When I reflect on the characteristics that produce rare human beings who inspire me, I wonder if their motivation for pressing forward was that they found something bigger than themselves to live for. What gave them the foresight and courage to leverage their all for the greater good? Human beings are inextricably connected to one another on this place we call home, Earth, and therefore, our destinies are locked together. Whatever happens, good or bad, in one part of town will eventually affect another part of town.

Civil Rights activist Fanny Lou Hamer, who reached the point of being "sick and tired of being sick and tired," was a regular, salt-of-the-earth, hard-working domestic, who sought to raise a family and live an ordinary life during the tumultuous 1960s. The injustice and brutality she and her fellow Mississippians experienced became so intolerable she had to respond. Her demand was simple: Equality, equity, and justice for all. She and those who looked like her—Black Americans—had grown tired and restless with accepting injustice and mediocrity. They wanted the same rights as all other Americans. Why was she able to see what many had grown blind to? What was the final straw that caused her to speak out against the injustices she had witnessed all her life? She and others reached a breaking point, a level of dissatisfaction so intense that settling for the status quo was no longer an option.

Fighting for the underdog—the lowest on the socio-economic ladder—and taking on the whole social order, was no small feat, yet she did it. While reading about her simple yet incredible testimony at the 1964 Democratic National Convention, and the inroads she carved for the Civil Rights Movement, I have gained a deep respect for her work and her words. I have often wondered if I would have had the same level of courage she did to face those challenges. I would like to think I would take the same courageous path she did. That makes me wonder if everyday people who respond to extraordinary challenges are born or developed. Perhaps it's both.

Being a student of history has allowed me to put life into context, to analyze current events, and to follow along the continuum that started generations ago. History goes all the way back to the beginning of time, and studying it allows an understanding of what is taking place now so we can respond to the nowness of life. I know of no better sanitizer than history to clarify the often-confusing realities we face in our current time. And with that clarity comes the call to action. We cannot just see more clearly; we have to do something about what we discover so future generations can avoid past mistakes and our children can pave a better way for their children, a path devoid of the murky mess we have all lived through.

All that has been lurking beneath the surface demands our attention. Ignorance and indifference do not provide plausible deniability or protection from reality. What we refuse to address will eventually gnaw away at us and ultimately consume us. It is time for a healing. That healing is necessary because many African Americans are psychologically damaged from our experience in America. Especially Black men. Me included. The world has become aware that America is more complicated than the façade it presents. Even recent immigrants have learned that. They might have once viewed this country as the land of milk and honey, a place filled with nothing but opportunity, because that is the story America exports to the world. They might have seen America as heaven on earth, a place where anything is possible when you work hard and obey the rules. However, that image of the American ideal has changed with the attacks on immigration witnessed in the last half decade. A knowledge of the historical influences on current events has a way of informing our perspective.

Author Isabel Wilkerson, in her book *Caste: The Origins of our Discontents*, states, "As American citizens, we are the stewards and heirs of a big, beautiful house." America can be viewed as a beautiful house, set up on a hill for all to aspire to and admire. At first glance, this house is inviting and beautiful, the picture of perfection that is shared globally. Below the surface, however, there are numerous infrastructure problems, coupled with an inferior foundation built upon inadequate soil. As the new stewards of this house that we occupy as Americans, we are all responsible for addressing the challenges that exist. That is our responsibility as beneficiaries of this American experiment. Just as a skilled neurosurgeon examines the x-rays before performing a delicate procedure, so must we look at the American experiment. We must drill beneath the surface to analyze what has created the confusion and discontent that every American citizen faces. The challenges we see are not someone else's. They belong to us all.

Some may say, "Do not burden me with this problem of race, equity, or justice. The ills of the past happened so very long ago.

Neither I nor any of my ancestors had anything to do with enslaving people, taking the land of our native brothers, or any other atrocities that may have occurred in the past." The truth is not one of us was here when the American house was being established, but the reality is that we are here today as beneficiaries and stewards. We have inherited what was established, whether that is good or bad, right or wrong. If we continue to ignore the challenges, we run the risk of being consumed by them all.

Most of the animosity that exists among the citizenry randomly appears like plumes of smoke from a simmering volcano. Some well-meaning and sincere people adopted the belief that the election of Barack Obama as President of the United States ushered in a post-racial era. How wrong they were. Had they been students of history, they would have known that any advancement achieved by a marginalized group is met with a contraction and a backlash. As such, America has experienced a striking increase in bigotry and racial violence in the twenty-first century. Now, this nation, viewed as the most successful democracy in the world, is faced with the decision to either continue down this destructive road littered with grief or improve upon the promise and ideals that extol opportunity for all.

This is not to suggest that everyone gets a first-place prize just for showing up. As with sports, pure sports, there is value in the egalitarian environment. I am grateful for the lessons I learned on and off the field. Having participated in sports for much of my young life, I learned that your gifts and talents, plus the effort you put forth to improve, ultimately determine your results. The same is true in America. There may have been some who hitched a free ride in society, but not many. Everyone has to earn their keep.

Our contemporary citizens did not create the original societal inequities and disparities. Still, it is our responsibility, as stewards of this land, to address and repair them, but stewardship must have at its foundation an understanding of the big picture. For many, that picture looks much different than it does for others.

For some Black people in America, that picture of a brighter future looks dim because marginalization has been experienced as the norm. That's the reason I do the work for those I serve— because there is a brighter future and there are opportunities for us all. Some of us have more obstacles to overcome than others do, but they can be overcome. The hope of Pro-Vision is that young men and women and the families and communities we serve come to know their history, to know who they are, to understand the forces and obstacles that they must navigate in order to achieve their hopes and dreams. I want them to know they have more knowledge and more power than they realize. They have what it takes to show up strong and achieve their dreams, despite any trauma they've experienced. They have what it takes to lead—themselves and their communities—so we all have a chance at more.

There are indigenous leaders throughout the community I serve. My goal is to awaken in them that call to service, the call to be a leader, but leadership is a responsibility that requires commitment to a vision bigger than one person. Leadership is about service to others. Many people want the external manifestations of leadership, but not the work and responsibility that come with them. An indisputable characteristic of leadership is responsibility. When I was a kid, my grandmother would send me to the store for whatever she needed that day. "Take this money and bring back some milk, rice, butter, and a loaf of bread," she'd say while handing me a rolled-up dollar bill or two. I would run off towards the corner grocery store as she stood on the porch watching me. I was given those instructions and put in the role of leadership, service, and responsibility. I knew what she expected of me and I did not want to disappoint her. I believed that if she trusted me to do that small task, maybe she would eventually trust me with something bigger. It was the beginning of my leadership journey.

Just like in the parable of the talents in Luke chapter 19, someone was entrusting me with something that I was responsible for returning. In that parable, a wealthy man was headed out of town for a while and wanted to make sure his property grew in value while he was away. He entrusted three of his servants with the responsibility to multiply the property he placed in their possession. One servant was given one talent, another received two talents, and one got five talents. When the wealthy man returned, he asked each of the servants to bring him the profits. The guy who was given the five talents brought back ten. The guy with the two talents brought back four, but the one who was given the one talent returned that same one talent and told the wealthy man that he decided to play it safe. "I know you're a hard man," the servant said to the wealthy man. "I didn't want to take any risks, so I dug a hole and put it in the ground. Here it is."

I can imagine the look on the wealthy man's face. What a disappointment. He ushered the other two servants into a celebration as a reward for their diligence and released the third one, saying, "I'm sorry. We no longer need your services. This assignment requires a responsible, conscientious person I can count on, but you didn't understand what I required of you."

There are some hard choices to make in leadership, and those choices often come with some risk. I have learned that throughout life and certainly in my role within Pro-Vision. I have risked making a wrong decision, trusting people who did not deserve it, or ignoring something that required my attention. A clear head, a solid view of the big picture of what I'm trying to accomplish, and an understanding of who I serve helps limit bad decisions, but I do not get the option of doing nothing. Leaders act. They get the information needed to move forward. They think things through, consult with advisors, and then they act, knowing that someone is always watching and taking notes. Leadership comes with the intrinsic result of being an example. Whether I like it or not, as a leader, I'm an example to those I lead. Every day, I have to decide what kind of example I want to be to those who are watching and learning from me, and then I have to walk in it.

The late, great Myles Munroe said that a good leader not only knows where they are going, but can also inspire others to go with them. That requires more than charisma; it takes integrity, character, and commitment, traits I have developed over time and through many missteps. I've had to transform the "my way or the highway" attitude and adopt a more thoughtful, patient, and nuanced approach. I've learned the use of the carrot versus the stick when relating to and inspiring others. I have evolved in all areas of leadership, and I now see my journey as that of an ordinary person with some latent gifts and talents, who accepted the call to lead others living in extraordinary circumstances into a place of self-efficacy and confidence. Like many others in leadership, I have to metaphorically fill my buckets—spiritual, mental, emotional, and physical—to remain healthy because the complexities and demands of leadership can be overwhelming.

As a leader, I do not get to determine what parts of my leadership persona those I lead decide to emulate. That is up to them. Some might see my leadership behavior and decide they want to replicate the way I speak to others, how I strategize, how I give and receive praise and criticism, or how I manage finances. I, as the leader, am merely an example of how it can be done. When I do everything to the best of my ability, those who observe me see the best I am as a leader. If I choose to shortcut any of it, I have no doubt that someone is watching that also. Because of my behavior and actions, they might get the message that skimping, cheating, lying, and similar behaviors are acceptable leadership actions they can replicate. That is not the kind of leadership behavior I want to exhibit or encourage. I want the young men and women watching me to see an ideal of leadership that impacts them in the way Uncle Nick, Coach Casem, Coach Audrich, my father, and others impacted me as a kid.

In some of the most nuanced ways, throughout my life and certainly in the thirty years I have led Pro-Vision, I've learned some valuable cornerstones of effective leadership. Among them is that you cannot be a leader if you have a bad relationship with money, a poor relationship with people, or a misunderstanding of the use of power that the position carries. The Creator has placed me in some unique spaces, where I can speak truth to power and try to influence resources to help people who are voiceless. That is one of the things that gives me the greatest joy. I have been around fame and I've been around fortune and people with it. Whether because of my humble upbringing or because of my experiences in the NFL, the fame and fortune don't impress me. I have remained myopic with my focus of the mission of Pro-Vision.

Some of our allies, as generous and genuine as they may have been, might not have been capable or prepared to assume a seat at Pro-Vision. This is a harsh reminder of the two Americas, a truth that is real for far too many of our fellow citizens. Anyone wishing to support Pro-Vision must first support the mission and not be indifferent to the realities of the people we serve and the disparities that impact their existence. Our allies must approach this work with a heart to understand the differences and challenges faced by the populations we serve, and then work to dismantle those disparities. Some do not understand that the issues are complex and, at times, inconvenient and downright uncomfortable. True allies have to be willing to be informed about the disparities that exist and know that these differences are real, not imagined. They must have a heart for people that listens and encourages. Not everyone has that capacity to address or overcome their own implicit prejudice and biases. Those who have come into this space with a cavalier attitude have not always served the mission properly. On the other hand, we are grateful that so many more have come to us with a servant's heart and an open mind.

I understand the condition of the community I serve, and I am keenly aware that I need allies with vision to help provide the resources to build housing and a farm and provide education for all the kids who need it. This authentic support understands the overwhelming need for character development programs that fill the chasm of reasonable adult supervision. Those who invest in Pro-Vision are not only investing in our vision and the families we serve; they are also investing in their own self-interest. They know what the benefits of a community like ours being self-reliant, sustainable, and a positive contributor to society at large can be.

When their seed transfers from their storehouse to ours, God is just rearranging resources to multiply them in the form of well-rounded young men and women poised to make a difference in the world. Those resources are seeds being planted inside communities where they are expected to thrive and grow through the commitment and contributions of the residents. Because those community residents come from a people who have historically made something out of nothing, they are endowed with the will and the power to turn something into something more.

From day one, Pro-Vision has focused on growing an organization that survives by the sweat of our own brow, by the input of those who benefit from our programs, and by the profit of the products we create. Once that self-reliance kicked in, I saw the benefit of it and realized that everything I need to live my purpose exists inside me. Everything our community needs is already here. Provided from those outside our community are support and encouragement for what we are already doing for ourselves. This does not mean we don't need other people to help, from time to time, because we do. What it means is that we understand nobody is going to do anything for us that we're not willing to do for ourselves. Donations we receive are welcomed and appreciated. They are seed money that I have the responsibility to reproduce for the good of the whole. In that sense, I see myself as the servant given five talents. It's my job to multiply what has been granted, so I can't be reckless with the gifts others have entrusted to me.

There is power and freedom in having the confidence to know my only currency is being true to the life I know I should be living. The Creator has charged me with the responsibility of spreading the good news to the underdog, just like Luke 4:18 states. To do this work, I have to decrease to allow my Creator to increase because it is by that power that things get done. Having sat in the seat of fame and released it, I see it for what it was, an entry point to discovering my purpose, not a defining moment in my life. I live to ignite and influence those who cross my path and to help the least of these see their value in this world.

The beauty of life is in the comfort and the peace that comes from being who you were created to be and setting a standard that clearly defines what success means to you. How open you are to your purpose determines how much time it takes for you to realize that purpose and do something constructive with it. Getting to that point is an individual journey that you must take because you will never be at peace unless you find out why you were created. Realizing my purpose has been the greatest joy of my life. It has enriched the lives of others, particularly through the institution I've been fortunate to steward, Pro-Vision.

My entire life journey and the work I do now are tributes to seeking and finding my purpose. In spite of who I am, and all my baggage and shortcomings, the Creator has chosen to funnel some goodness through me. Each moment I realize that, I am humbled because, although some see me as a hard-charging community leader, I am still that eleven-year-old kid who was the underdog. Only now, I have the courage to journey the road less traveled. I am not waiting for others to validate me. Walking in the shadow of footsteps has allowed me to find my purpose, the reason I exist in this world. That is a journey worth taking.

Acknowledgments

The old saying, "You don't know what you don't know" was never truer for me than when I set out on my voyage to write this book. Not only did I not know what I was doing or what to expect when writing a book, I had no idea the direction my story would take. In full disclosure, I was a proud procrastinator when it came to sitting down to write. To my advantage, that procrastination allowed an amazing team of people into my sphere to guide me along this unchartered journey. The only serious thoughts I put forth regarding the manuscript early on were moments when my beautiful wife, Kathleen and I would reflect on our life journey together. Those moments became precious time spent. Thank you, Kathleen.

To my mother, Joyce Davis Young and my late father Wallace Young Sr., thank you for loving and caring about me enough to provide the discipline and encouragement I needed to meet my destiny. To my late grandmother, Stella Gibbs, for giving me her unconditional love, for making me feel like I was special, and for instilling in me the faith and strength of the ancestors who left a rich legacy. Thank you to Diana Seifert, the Executive Director of Pro-Vision, Inc., who oversees the day-to-day operations. Big things come in small packages, and Diana is the personification of that notion. She is a fearless Pro-Vision champion. Thank you for driving me to cross the finish line with this book and with everything we endeavor to accomplish at Pro-Vision on behalf of the least of those in our society.

As I reflected on my childhood while writing this manuscript, I thought often of my late sister, Whylene "Pie" Young. Many say she was a female version of me, in temperament and in her take-charge attitude. She was a force of nature. Everyone who knew her loved her, and we all miss her greatly. My heartfelt thanks goes to all my siblings for their love and support: Michelle Young Frazier, Valerie Young Vaughn, Brian Young, Dernell Young, and Wallace Young Jr. To the Creator be the glory!

No one makes it through life without some coaching, formal or informal. I have been blessed to have some of the most incredible coaches in my life, each of whom influenced me more than they will ever know, both in football and in life: James Audrich and Leroy Walker, my high school football coaches, who guided me and provided the foundation I needed both on and off the field; Marino Casem, my college football coach, who was a force of nature and what I needed at that point in my life; Dick Vermeil of the Philadelphia Eagles, who baptized me into the NFL, thank you for allowing me to view true leadership.

I appreciate the following individuals, who were special "coaches" and crossed my path through my work at Pro-Vision: Carrie Tate, for standing in the gap all those years at Pro-Vision; Kenneth Patrick ("KP"), for being one of the three young men who helped launch Pro-Vision on that fateful Saturday morning; Dr. Janell James, for consistently being a coach, mentor, and supporter; Dr. Roderick Paige, for introducing Pro-Vision into the educational arena in 1995; Dr. Warner Ervin, for his integrity, great counsel, and support; and all the outstanding Pro-Vision board members, current and past. Thank you to the Pro-Vision staff, who show up daily and work hard to fulfill the mission. A special thanks to all the other unbelievable human beings who invest in the lives of others through Pro-Vision with their time, talents, or treasures.

Thanks to my collaborative writing partner, Anita Henderson, and to my editor, Candice L. Davis. A special thanks to Janice McNair, without whom this book would never have taken flight. Thank you for your persistence and staying on me to get this book done. Thank you to Leslie Frazier, Dr. Roderick Paige, and Jamie Roots for your support and endorsements. Ron Smith, thank you for your undying support as a friend, confidant and sounding board, and for being a positive influence in my life. Melinda Spaulding, thank you for believing in me, for believing in Pro-Vision, and for sharing your talents. Thanks to Marvin Pierre, Isabela Gonzalez, Diane Maben, Ron Smith, Janelle James, and Ja'Corey Miller for reading an early version of this manuscript and sharing your feedback. This book was designed for you.

About the Author

Roynell Young, former Philadelphia Eagles All-Pro Cornerback, is Founder and CEO of Pro-Vision, Inc., a nonprofit he's had the privilege of stewarding since 1990 with a vision for developing Houston's often forgotten and overlooked young people. Young was selected from Alcorn State University in the first round of the 1980 NFL Draft. He enjoyed a nine-year career in the National Football  League with the Eagles before retiring in 1988 to pursue his passion for youth and community development.

Once retired, he spent months searching for how he could serve young people, particularly those engaging in behaviors that were counterproductive and destructive to their future. With that goal in mind, he founded Pro-Vision, Inc., which has since evolved into an organization that has made a notable impact on Houston's Sunnyside community and beyond. Pro-Vision's approach to youth and community development includes four parts: character development, education, nutrition, and safe, affordable housing. The extraordinary results of the work at Pro-Vision demonstrates Young's vision for a self-sustainable, child-centered, adult-governed, and elderly-ruled community. As a product of the uptown neighborhood of New Orleans, Louisiana, that was the kind of community that nurtured Young as a child. Throughout his life, he has desired to provide a similar safety net for those who are here and those who are yet to be born.

As a result of his work, Young was chosen by the U.S. State Department to lead a televised conference in Bosnia, in 2010, on how to work with disenchanted male youth. He delivered the 2010 keynote address at the National Conference on Juvenile Justice hosted by the National Council of Juvenile and Family Court Judges. Young was recognized for his work by former Governor Rick Perry, former U.S. Secretary of Education Rod Paige, former City Councilmember and current Member of the U.S. Congress Sheila Jackson Lee, U.S. Congressman Al Green, and former U.S. Congressman Chris Bell. His life is an example of how responsible adults can make a meaningful impact on the lives of young people.

Young received a bachelor of science degree from Alcorn State University and is a Senior Fellow of the Houston Chapter of the American Leadership Forum, Educational Class II. In recognition of his work at Pro-Vision, Young has received numerous awards, including the 2010 Texas Women's Empowerment Foundation Community Mentor Award, the 2010

Mentoring Award presented by the Houston Metropolitan Chapter of 100 Black Men, Inc., the 2008 Community Service Award from Pan-African Orthodox Christian Church, Who's Who 2007, Unsung Hero Award of 2004, the Savvy Award presented by Foley's and the *Houston Chronicle*, the KTRK-ABC Houston Community Service Award, and the AM 740 Everyday Hero Award. Roynell Young and the Pro-Vision story have been featured in *The New York Times*, *Time for Kids*, *Guideposts* magazine, and *Men's Journal*, among other national news platforms. Locally, features have run in the *Houston Chronicle*, as well as the CBS, ABC, and Fox26 networks.

In 2017, Young was inducted into the Southwestern Athletic Conference (SWAC) Hall of Fame for the contributions he made to SWAC athletics as a student-athlete, coach, and administrator. In 2021, Young was inducted into the Black College Football Hall of Fame. He lives near Houston, Texas, with his wife, Kathleen, and is the proud father of Roynell Young Jr.

CPSIA information can be obtained
at www.ICGtesting.com
Printed in the USA
LVHW071924120921
697662LV00016B/717/J

9 781737 728436